Planning and Control
for IT Services

IT Infrastructure Library

Dave Ruffles
Colin Hebden
Nigel Cresswell

Office of Government Commerce

LONDON: THE STATIONERY OFFICE

First published by HMSO 1994
Sixth impression published by The Stationery
Office 2001

ISBN	0 11 330548 6
ISSN	0956–2591

OGC – the Office of Government Commerce – is
an office of HM Treasury. Set up in 2000, it
incorporates the Central Computer and
Telecommunications Agency (CCTA), which will
no longer operate as a separate agency.

The OGC is now the authority for best practice in
commercial activities in UK government,
combining a number of separate functions with
related aims.

OGC will build on the popular guidance
developed by the former CCTA and others,
working with organisations internationally to
develop and share business and practitioner
guidance within a world-class best practice.

This is one of the books published in the IT
Infrastructure Library series.

For further information on OGC products, contact:

OGC Library,
Rosebery Court,
St Andrews Business Park
NORWICH NR7 0HS

Telephone 01603 704930   GTN 30404930

This document has been produced using
procedures conforming to
BSI 5750 Part 1: 1987; ISO 9001:1987.

Table of contents

Annexes

Foreword

Welcome to the IT Infrastructure Library module on
Planning and Control for IT Services.

In their respective areas the IT Infrastructure Library
publications complement and provide more detail than the
IS Guides.

The ethos behind the development of the IT Infrastructure
Library is the recognition that organizations are becoming
increasingly dependent on IT in order to satisfy their
corporate aims and meet their business needs. This growing
dependency leads to growing requirement for quality
IT services. In this context quality means 'matched to
business needs and user requirements as these evolve'.

This module is one of a series of codes of practice intended
to facilitate the quality management of IT services and of
the IT Infrastructure. (By IT Infrastructure, we mean
organizations' computers and networks - hardware,
software and computer related communications, upon
which application systems and IT services are built and
run). The codes of practice will assist organizations to
provide quality IT services in the face of skill shortages,
system complexity, rapid change, growing user
expectations, current and future user requirements.

Underpinning the IT Infrastructure is the Environmental
Infrastructure upon which it is built. Environmental topics
are covered in separate sets of guides within the
IT Infrastructure Library.

IT service management is a complex subject which for
presentational and practical reasons has been broken down
within the IT Infrastructure Library into a series of modules.
A complete list of current and planned modules is available
from the CCTA IT Infrastructure Management Services at
the address given at the back of this module.

Consistency versus new challenges

The IT Infrastructure Library has been produced over a
period of five years during which there have been
significant changes in the business environment of Central
Government. Major initiatives such as Next Steps, Citizen's
Charter and Competing for Quality are affecting the
organization of Departments and the way in which they
conduct their business. These changes are having a
significant effect on the IT Directorate.

The production of later volumes of the IT Infrastructure Library has therefore presented the dual challenges of maintaining consistency with earlier publications while ensuring relevance to today's Government departments. Both the changes in the Government department business environment and latest thinking in IT service management need to be taken into account. For example, the impact of market testing is addressed in the later books, even though the Competing for Quality White Paper had not been issued when the early books were published.

Some of the challenges which IT service suppliers face are:

* meeting requirements specified by the customer

* improved timeliness of response to customer needs

* cutting costs to provide economic, competitively priced services

* a clear separation of supply (provider of services) and demand (customer of services) with defined interfaces, regardless of whether or not the supply is in-house

* devolution of authority and budgets enabling the customer to decide which IT service suppliers to use.

Many of these issues have been identified and addressed in earlier volumes of the IT Infrastructure Library. However, changes in the business environment have provided new focus and emphasis which is particularly evident in this and other recent volumes. Further information is available in CCTA's Market Testing IS/IT publications.

Common themes and relationships in the IT Infrastructure Library

Three closely related modules in the Managers' Set of the IT Infrastructure Library provide additional information about common themes which run through all other modules in the Library: IT Services Organization, Planning and Control for IT Services and Quality Management for IT Services. These books give three different viewpoints or ways of looking at the IT Services organization:

* **IT Services Organization** concentrates on organizational structure, describes roles, skills and experience required by people, and provides a framework for reviewing the organizational structure to meet changing circumstances

* **Planning and Control for IT Services** covers information flows and the development of an appropriate planning and control system to meet the requirements of the organization; people are one of the resources to be considered and the organizational structure will influence information flows, but the module has a wider focus covering all aspects of planning and control

* **Quality Management for IT Services** is concerned with putting in place an ISO9001 conformant quality management system; it encompasses organizational and planning and control aspects, since they are covered by the ISO9001 standard, but refers to the above two modules rather than repeating information.

In general, the three modules answer the following questions:

* who and where?

  - IT Services Organization

* what and when?

  - Planning and Control for IT Services

* what, why and how?

  - Quality Management for IT Services.

The three modules address distinct but closely related aspects of IT service management. Organizations using the IT Infrastructure Library may choose to use the three modules as part of a coordinated project. In particular, changes to organizational structure and the development of planning and control processes will often need to be considered in parallel. In addition, many organizations seek to develop procedures in line with the ISO9001 quality management standard which covers organizational issues and the use of plans and controls, but has a wider scope and refers to policies and standards, detailed procedures, agreements with the customer and document control.

The close links between the subject matters of these three modules, and indeed with others in the Library, means that there is a degree of overlap. Nevertheless these three modules present different but valid viewpoints of managing IT Services.

The structure of the module is, in essence:

* a **Management summary** aimed at senior managers (Directors of IT and above, typically down to Civil Service Grade 5), senior IT staff and, in some cases, users or office managers (typically Civil Service Grades 5 to 7)

* the main body of the text, aimed at IT middle management (typically grades 7 to HEO)

* technical detail in Annexes.

The module gives the main **guidance** in sections 3 to 5; explains the **benefits, costs and possible problems** in section 6, which may be of interest to senior staff; and provides information on **tools** (requirements and examples of real-life availability) in section 7.

CCTA is working with the IT industry to foster the development of software tools to underpin the guidance contained within the codes of practice (ie to make adherence to the module more practicable), and ultimately to automate functions.

If you have any comments on this or other modules, do please let us know. A **Comments sheet** is provided with every module. Alternatively you may wish to contact us directly using the reference point given in **Further information**.

Thank you. We hope you find this module useful.

Acknowledgement

The assistance of the following contributors is gratefully acknowledged:

Colin Hebden and Nigel Cresswell (under contract to CCTA from EDS Scicon Ltd).

1. Management summary

The pressures on organizations' IT providers to satisfy their customers' business needs through the delivery of quality IT services has never been greater. Whether the business drivers are:

*   to reduce costs

*   to gain competitive edge which, in the public sector, could mean the ability to bid competitively against private sector service providers in a market testing exercise

*   to increase market share

*   to provide services to enable the business to fulfil its business needs including such things as meeting Citizens Charter requirements.

IT service providers must plan proactively to deliver the quality of service required. Only in this way will they position themselves to achieve these business goals.

Effective planning and control is a pre-requisite for the successful management of any venture. The information in this module will help organizations manage the provision of services, referred to here as Information Technology (IT) services, which support a business through the use of IT systems (computers, networks, etc). This module provides guidance on how to establish and sustain a planned and controlled environment for the provision of IT services.

1.1 The importance of IT services

The effective delivery of IT services to an organization's business community is closely linked to how effectively its IT Services Organization is managed. Meeting cost, time and functionality targets is paramount and a reactive, unplanned approach to IT service provision will almost certainly have a negative impact on the customers, the parent organization and the IT Services Organization itself. The only effective approach is to operate proactive planning and control.

This module is part of the CCTA's IT Infrastructure Library. Like other modules in the library, it addresses IT service provision which is an on-going activity. In this respect, the management of IT service provision differs in character from planning and controlling a single finite project, which has a clear beginning and end, although conducting such projects will be a part of IT service provision when existing services are extended and new services introduced.

The delivery and management of operational IT services, and management of the IT infrastructure on which those services are run are referred to collectively as service management. The organizational group responsible for service management is the IT Services Organization.

The effectiveness of the management of IT service provision, and of the IT Services Organization in delivering those services, determines how well they can meet their customers' business needs and, consequently, how well the business objectives can be met.

1.2 The aim of planning and control

The aim of planning and control is to provide information to ensure that IT services are provided as specified, to time and within budget. Planning and control should be treated as a total, coherent and logical set of activities which may be carried out across physical boundaries such as internal organizational structures, separate companies, or a number of individuals. It is important to look at the whole process to ensure that it is complete and consistent across boundaries. There is much talk about virtual organizations - this module describes planning and control for a virtual organization.

This module recommends the use of planning and control within the framework of a Quality Management System (QMS). However, the guidance in this module is relevant to all organizations whether they have a QMS or not.

1.3 The changing scenario

As the foreword to this book explains, a number of events have impacted upon the provision of IT services within government organizations which have resulted in a range of possible customer/service supplier scenarios. To give advice which covered all possible scenarios would be difficult to achieve so this module has been written from the point of view of in-house provision. This presents the most simple scenario where planning and control can be integrated and more easily coordinated.

If parts of the IT Directorate have been outsourced, including IT service provision, then relationships must be established to ensure that information exchange occurs, as specified and required here, between the customer organization and external service providers and that activities are carried out by the appropriate organization. For example, if IT service provision is outsourced the external organization must have an understanding of the IT strategy of the customer organization. If application development has also been outsourced, and an external service provider is expected to take on and run the live services using these applications, then a dialogue must be set up between the two outsourced service providers. As there are a large number of possible scenarios for outsourcing the reader must determine how best to interpret this guidance for their own situation.

If service management has been outsourced the customer organization should ensure that the provider has appropriate plans and controls to ensure that the customer is provided with the information required and that resources are being managed, since the customer will be paying for this.

1.4 Planning

Planning is the process of defining a sequence of activities to achieve stated objectives. Scheduling is the assignment of actual resources and start and completion dates within the planning task.

There is a hierarchy of planning activities defined by the timescale in which they take place.

Strategic planning considers the wider, long-term view and sets the direction.

Tactical planning identifies the medium term, specific actions that will move the organization in the desired direction.

Operational planning deals with the detail of implementing these specific actions in the short term.

Plans are usually required for each business unit in an organization. Business change programmes arising from new ventures must also be planned and businesses often set out strategic plans for critical subjects such as Information Systems. The IT Services Organization must reconsider its own strategic direction as a result of these changes.

Planning the provision of IT services must be fully integrated with all relevant aspects of business planning if business objectives are to be efficiently and effectively met. To this end, business and IT people must work together on the relevant plans, with the levels of service agreed between customer and service provider being formally documented as Service Level Agreements. However, if the service provider is market tested, and the IT services outsourced, the relationship between customer and service provider would be a contractual one. The proactive management of that relationship should ensure a win/win situation in that both the IT Services Organization's and its customers' business objectives are met.

1.5 Control

Control is the process of ensuring that the objectives are achieved.

Establishing workable plans is one aspect of creating a well managed environment. Managers must also monitor the planned activities, and control progress through corrective action and the modification of plans when necessary. Formal management reporting is one of the keys to carrying out this process. The IT Services Organization must report service capability and performance to its customers and to the business and IS planning teams. This ensures that future planning takes full account of IT service issues.

1.6 Benefits

The implementation of a system to plan and control the provision of IT services will help any IT Services Organization to support the successful achievement of the appropriate business driver(s) identified at 1 above. In addition, there are benefits to be gained by different parts of an organization from the introduction of planning and control in the IT Services Organization.

The main benefits should be:

* to the parent organization

    - greater efficiency and effectiveness through better informed planning of future requirements for IT service provision

    - reduced costs

* to the customers

    - improved delivery of the required levels of IT service

    - more effective response to new IT service requirements

* to the IT Service Management Team, improved information with which to

    - manage change better

    - improve their own effectiveness and efficiency.

2. Introduction

2.1 Purpose of the module

This module is about planning and control to support the delivery of IT services which meet the business needs of an organization. The module provides guidance on the practices and procedures necessary for the effective planning and control of IT services.

Planning is setting out a course of action to meet a goal; control is ensuring that the goal is attained. Having effective plans and controls in place helps to:

* achieve effective direction, allocation and prioritization of resources

* identify effects which might lead to failure to meet the overall goals and responsibilities of the IT Services Organization

* provide informative reports of current and future performance.

In this module we use the term parent organization to describe the wider business organization, for example a government department, of which the IT Directorate is a part, along with the various areas that are its customers.

2.1.1 What are IT services?

An IT service, for the purposes of this module, is taken to relate to operational IT services, ie the provision, operation and maintenance of IT infrastructure, enabling access to information systems, applications and data to customers' business specification, in support of one or more business areas. It is perceived by the customer of the service as a coherent and self contained entity. An IT service may:

* range from access to a single application (such as a general ledger system) to a complex set of facilities including many applications

* be provided from a central system or, as is the case with office automation, could be spread across a number of hardware and software platforms.

An organization's IT services are supported by the IT infrastructure which is comprised of hardware, software, and computer related communications.

The management objective for the IT Services Organization is to deliver and support IT services that meet their customers' business needs in a cost effective way using the IT infrastructure. This means that all operational IT activities must support the continuing strategic, tactical and operational requirements of the customer business in the most efficient manner possible.

This module recognizes the importance of planning and controlling the delivery of IT services within the context of IS planning. IS takes the wider view of the organization's information processing and addresses both the manual and the IT services treatment of information. Organizations need to formulate a strategy for IS which is consistent with their own business plans. IT can effectively contribute to business objectives only if IT planners and implementors work in the context of the business plans and the IS strategy.

A prerequisite for planning IT services is, therefore, a sound relationship with the organization's business and IS planning functions, in order that IT services meet the ever changing needs of business on a continuing basis.

Delivery of IT services is achieved through the application of resources, notably the IT infrastructure and people in the IT Services Organization. Managers must plan the use of these resources in line with the goals set and then direct and control their performance.

2.1.2 Allocating time to planning and control

A substantial proportion of the total work load for IT Services Organization managers covers routine operation including dealing with problems and requests for change from users. Much of the remaining effort is for involvement in service and infrastructure improvement programmes. In this situation, finding time for planning and controlling the use of resources is often difficult, but experience shows that it will ultimately reduce the amount of management time spent on dealing with crises. The net effect will be a better service to customers and a more pleasant working environment.

Successful IT service delivery depends on both planning and control. The potential for incurring extra costs by not adopting formal planning and control is greater in large organizations but this can be a problem for all organizations.

2.2   Target readership

The IT Infrastructure Library provides guidance for those
with managerial responsibility and accountability for IT
services. This module is written for IT Directors, IT Service
Managers and all IT staff with responsibilities for
supporting the Planning and Control function, such as the
IT Planning Unit.

However, much of the guidance is equally applicable to
planning and control of any service, not just IT. Guidance is
often kept as general, and only related specifically to IT
where necessary. The module should, therefore, also be of
use to managers in other fields.

2.3   Scope

This module is about planning and control in an IT Services
Organization. The module shows how the plans for the
provision of IT services should be developed from the
business and IS plans. It also shows the need to coordinate
and integrate with existing operational plans.

The module gives guidance on the:

* procedures necessary for effective planning and
  control

* relationships between IT Services Organization's
  plans

* reports necessary for effective management

* process of preparing, implementing and then
  maintaining an effective planning and control
  system, giving the

  - procedures required

  - dependencies on other activities

  - people involved

  - timing of the introduction.

The module covers the key aspects of the successful
introduction of effective planning and control for IT service
provision as part of an overall Quality Management System
(QMS) as described in the CCTA Quality Management
Library. This module is written as if organizations had little
or no planning and control in place, although in reality all
organizations will have some. However, even where a

significant level of planning and control exists, managers should find the module useful for reviewing and augmenting existing procedures.

Section 3

The basic concepts of planning and control, and a functional framework for the management of IT service provision, are introduced in section 3. More detail is given in Annex B (basic concepts) and Annex F (functional framework). Section 3 also deals with:

* the iterative nature of planning and control activities

* the need for liaison with the business and IS planning processes

* how an IT Services Organization should plan for and justify a new planning and control system

* the importance of management commitment to the introduction of a planning and control system

* the need to involve the IT Services Organization's staff and customers.

Section 4

Provides guidance on how to introduce or improve the planning and control process in an organization. It describes how the IT Services Organization's plans, policies and reports relate to the business and IS plans. The set of relevant documents is listed in Annex D and examples are contained in Annex E.

Section 5

Provides guidance on post-implementation activities. These embrace the review and maintenance of the plans, the use of controls to influence management action and the audit of the planning and control system itself.

Section 6

Benefits and costs of an effective planning and control system, and some of the problems likely to be encountered, are summarized in this section.

Section 7

Some indication of the tools available to help managers and planners develop, maintain and control their plans is given in section 7.

Section 8

Contains a bibliography for those wishing to read further into the subject.

The annexes provide a wealth of information to complement sections 3-5; the information is removed from in-line text to aid readability, but many of the annexes are essential reading for a full understanding of the planning and control processes.

Annex A   Contains a glossary of terms used in the module.

Annex B   Describes the basic concepts of planning and control in an organization.

Annex C   Summarizes CCTA's guidance on planning for Information Systems.

Annexes D&E   Describe the documents that are concerned with planning and control for IT services.

Annex F   Contains a directory of functional groups and explains the broad functions of those groups. The functions have been grouped because they carry out similar or related activities and have been grouped together only to assist in the production of this book. They do not depict a CCTA preferred organizational framework.

2.4   Related guidance

This module is one of a series that constitutes the CCTA IT Infrastructure Library. Although the module can be read in isolation, it is recommended that it is used in conjunction with other modules. The module contains generic guidance on planning and control for IT service provision. It gives advice on what areas need planning and control and how they interact. For detailed guidance on individual functions within the IT Services Organization, the relevant IT Infrastructure Library module should be consulted.

Implicit reference is made to:

*   all IT Infrastructure Library modules

*   the CCTA Quality Management Library

*   the CCTA IS Guides, particularly A2 - Strategic Planning for Information Systems

*   the CCTA IS Planning Subject Guides, particularly The Role of the IT Planning Unit.

2.5   Standards

No standards have been identified that relate specifically to planning and control of IT service provision. However, the following have some relevance.

ISO9001/EN29001/BS5750 Part 1 - Quality Management and Quality Assurance Standards

The IT Infrastructure Library modules are designed to assist adherents, for example organizations' IT Directorates, to obtain third-party quality certification to ISO9001. Such third parties should be accredited by the NACCB, the National Accreditation Council for Certification Bodies.

PRINCE Project Management Method

PRINCE is the recommended CCTA method for project management. All major initiatives should be planned and implemented using PRINCE. These include:

* projects to extend IT services and IT infrastructure

* the introduction of a planning and control system.

CRAMM

CRAMM is the recommended CCTA method for analyzing and managing the risks associated with an information system. A guide to interfacing CRAMM and PRINCE is available from CCTA.

3. Planning to implement planning and control in the IT Services Organization

This section of the module provides guidance on the processes required to prepare to implement planning and control in an IT Services Organization, including:

* the steps involved in preparing (3.1)

* the dependencies (3.2)

* the people involved (3.3)

* timing issues (3.4).

The section starts by outlining the context for planning and control in an IT Services Organization and the concepts behind the methods for planning and control:

* context for planning and control in the IT Services Organization(3.0.1)

* typical functions within the IT Services Organization (3.0.2)

* interfaces with IS and business planning and how business requirements are converted into the IT Services Organization's plans (3.0.3)

* planning process for the IT Services Organization(3.0.4)

* control mechanisms and management reporting in the IT Services Organization(3.0.5).

3.0 Context and concepts

3.0.1 Context for the IT Services Organization's planning and control

Planning and control of IT services takes place within a parent organization. A general picture of the pressures and processes, both inside and outside the organization, which influence planning and control is given in figure 1. A more detailed picture of the process is given in figure 2.

Figures 1 and 2 illustrate the context for planning and control in the IT Services Organization as recommended in the IT Infrastructure Library.

Figure 1

Figure 1 shows how the organization's Management Board relates to the external environment and provides direction and purpose to the organization. The organization's external environment has three components:

* **its purpose**, defined by the owners (the government or local authority in the case of a public sector department or a private company's shareholders)

* **the immediate business setting**, governed by the broader business environment, which includes economic factors, customer needs, competitive pressures, and, in the case of government departments, possible Citizen's Charter requirements, etc

* **relevant regulations, standards and advice** produced by regulatory authorities and other agencies.

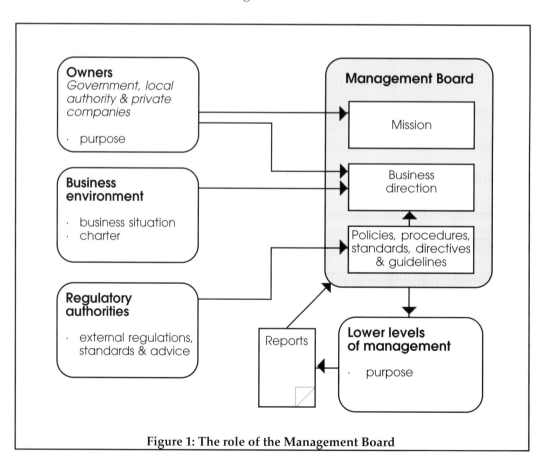

Figure 1: The role of the Management Board

The purpose is usually converted by the Management Board into a mission statement, a succinct summary of why the organization exists. This mission statement, together with an analysis of the current and forecast business situation, is used to define business direction. This is usually expressed as measurable objectives, and supported by policies, procedures, standards and guidelines. These in turn refer to external regulations, standards and advice. Together, these form the purpose for lower levels of management.

This process of defining the purpose repeats throughout the organization. At each hierarchical level, reports on achievement against the purpose must be provided for the level above.

Figure 2

Figure 2 illustrates how business managers, IS planners (governed by the IS Steering Committee, the ISSC) and programme directors, translate the Management Board's directives into purpose and direction for the managers of IT services.

Business managers develop business plans for their respective areas of responsibility which are likely to require IT services. These plans must be agreed by both business managers and the IT Directorate, particularly the IT Services Organization. Where the delivery of IT service has been outsourced the Service Control Team(SCT) will be responsible for agreeing the changes to the requirement with the service provider. The agreed requirements are encapsulated as Service Level Agreements (SLAs). Further information on the role of an SCT is contained in the IT Infrastructure Library **Managing Facilities Management** module.

Some business plans require co-operation across business areas and these should be formed into business programmes. CCTA recommends the appointment of a Programme Board and Programme Director for each programme.

An Information Systems (IS) strategy in support of business needs should be developed by an IS Steering Committee (ISSC). The ISSC should be led by business managers and requires the involvement of the IT Directorate. The IS strategy provides an overall framework for business plans and business programmes which affect those business processes which rely on information.

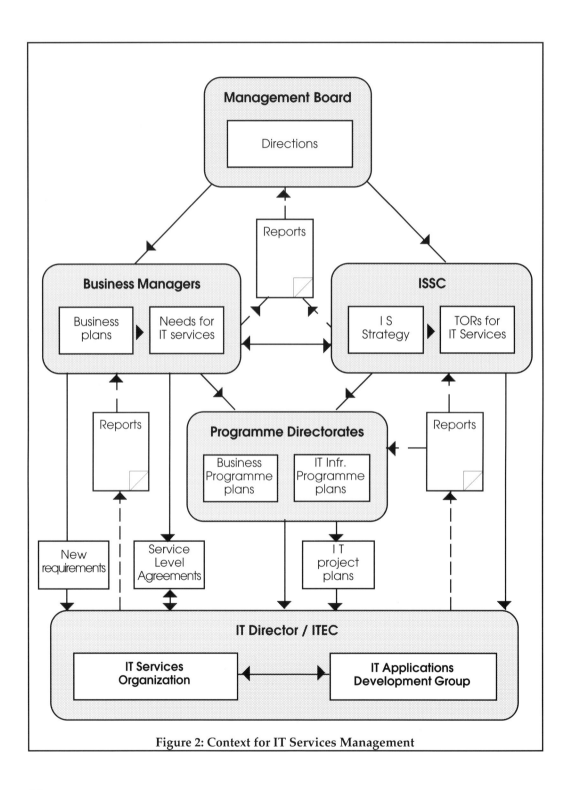

Figure 2: Context for IT Services Management

The IS strategy may require changes in the IT infrastructure, and lead to an IT infrastructure programme.

The main elements determining the purpose of the IT Services Organization are:

* the project plans which emerge from business and IT infrastructure programmes

* new requirements for IT services

* SLAs

* terms of reference set by the ISSC.

The IT Services Organization normally exists as part of an IT Directorate, which also contains an Applications Development Group responsible for developing new applications software. Liaison between the IT Services Organization and the Applications Development Group is essential in planning and controlling IT service provision. More information on this liaison is contained in the IT Infrastructure Library **Software Lifecycle Support** module.

However, the increasing programme of market testing within Government IT will mean changes in the composition of IT Directorates. Organizations will need to plan to retain effective control of the services provided to them where they are provided by external sources, see the IT Infrastructure Library **Managing Facilities Management** module.

3.0.2 The IT Services Organization

The delivery and management of operational IT services, and management of the IT infrastructure on which those services run, are referred to collectively as service management. The organizational group responsible for service management is the IT Services Organization.

This section of the module describes a functional framework (NB this is not an organizational framework) underpinning an IT Services Organization and its environment. The framework is illustrated in figure 3. Each function consists of a group of related activities, and fulfils a role in specifying, using, delivering or supporting IT services. It may be inside or outside the IT Services Organization. Functions which fulfil similar or related roles are grouped together in the figure.

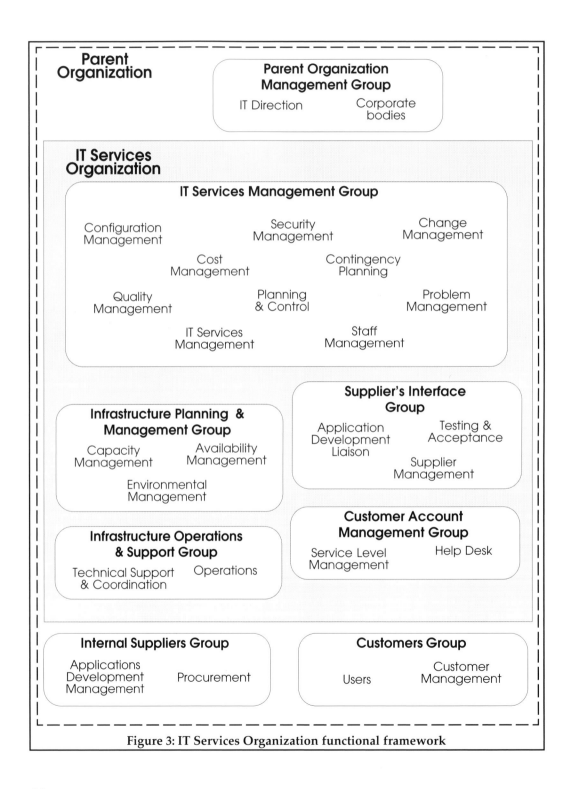

Figure 3: IT Services Organization functional framework

Where possible, the names of the functions correspond to the titles of modules in the IT Infrastructure Library. This has not been possible where:

* an IT Infrastructure Library module addresses a general subject such as Customer Liaison and Software Lifecycle Support

* functions in the framework cover more than one IT Infrastructure Library title - Operations, for example covers networks, central processing and operation of distributed and local equipment.

The grouping of functions in the framework does not necessarily reflect organizational structure, but in many cases there will be a close match between functional groups and the organizational hierarchy. Organizational structure is addressed in the IT Infrastructure Library **IT Services Organization** module.

Separate functions in the framework do not necessarily correspond to individual posts in the IT Services Organization. Depending on the nature of the function, the scale of the organization and on other local factors, a function may either be fulfilled by a team of individuals or by one individual who may cover other functions as well. Similarly, a manager may be responsible for one or more functions. This view of a function is consistent with the guidance in the rest of IT Infrastructure Library.

External functions

The framework does not include one group of functions which is entirely outside the IT Services Organization and its parent organization. This group includes external suppliers and the various regulatory and standards bodies which affect the provision of IT services. These bodies include the Health and Safety Executive, the Data Protection Registrar, and BS5750 and NACCB/NAMAS certification bodies.

Three other groups - Customers, Parent Organization Management and Internal Suppliers - involve activities conducted within the parent organization but usually outside the IT Services Organization itself but which it needs to consider during its own planning and control activity.

Internal functions

Inside the IT Services Organization are the functions responsible for providing IT services to its customers. Some functions perform management, planning, controlling and directing roles; others are involved more directly in service provision.

Planning and control activities exist in all of the functions within the IT Services Organization to some extent. Ultimately, the IT Services Manager is responsible, inter alia, for planning and control within the IT Services Organization, but an administrative Planning and Control function has been identified which may be delegated if required. (See section 3.1.4 for details of the key roles of this function.)

The service delivery chain from the IT Services Organization to its customers is made up of five groups. The first provides the overall management of the IT Services Management Organization; three provide, maintain and operate the IT infrastructure; the fifth provides services directly to customers.

The functions involved in sustaining the infrastructure, thereby providing the service delivery chain, are grouped into:

* IT Services Management Group - responsible for overall management of the IT Services Organization

* Suppliers Interface group - deals directly with external suppliers

* Infrastructure Planning and Management group - responsible for planning and managing the infrastructure

* Infrastructure Operations and Support group - operate the infrastructure directly

* Customer Account Management group

   - ensure that IT services are provided to the level required by the customer

   - manages and provides all aspects of the interface with customers.

More information on this functional framework can be found in Annex F.

3.0.3 Interfaces with business and IS planning

Planning and control in the IT Services Organization are driven by business direction, ie increasing efficiency by reducing costs, gaining competitive edge and increasing market share, and additionally, in the public sector, by market testing and fulfilling Citizens Charter requirements. See section 3.0.1 and Annexes B and C for a description of these basic concepts. Further guidance is also available in a range of CCTA and other publications (see section 8, Bibliography).

The key documents which define the IT Services Organization's purpose fall into three main groups:

* mission statement

* plans and requirements

* policies, procedures, standards and guidelines.

Brief information about these groups is given here. More detailed information is given in Annex B, section B.3. The various planning activities are described in Annexes B and C. More information on the documents is to be found in Annex D, sections D.1 and D.2.

Mission

The mission for the IT Services Organization is set by the parent organization (normally by the IS Steering Committee if one exists) and passed through the IT Director. It may be part of a Terms of Reference document or may be a single mission statement.

Plans and requirements

The primary sources of plans and requirements are the parent organization's business plans. The process of planning for IS and IT infrastructure develops these business plans into:

* IS Strategy Study Report

* financial provisions

* programme plans and requirements for changes to applications systems and the IT infrastructure

* infrastructure project requirements and plans.

Services required by customers may also be defined in existing SLAs. If SLAs do not exist they should be developed and agreed with the relevant customers as described in the IT Infrastructure Library **Service Level Management** module. The SLAs form part of the total set of plans and requirements for IT services.

Service and product suppliers will also provide relevant information in the form of catalogues.

Policies, procedures, standards & guidelines

The IT Services Organization will be expected to conform to policies, procedures, standards and guidelines set by:

* the parent organization (in a Corporate Policies and Procedures Manual)

* national and/or international regulatory bodies affecting security, health and safety, procurement, standards and data protection

* advisory bodies such as CCTA - their advice is based on recommended best practice.

3.0.4 IT Services Organization planning

Provision of IT services involves many activities that are carried out on a more or less continuous basis, with no, or only a few, identifiable milestones or end dates. This makes it difficult to apply project management techniques to managing IT services. However, objectives including improvement targets for IT service provision, related to timescales, can be identified from the purpose, plans and requirements that have been laid down. From these objectives, it should be possible to estimate resource needs, develop IT Services Organization's plans and track progress against the plans. The measurement of progress or operational performance will essentially be driven by customer needs as contained in statements of service requirements. However, as with the management of any business, measurements will be required of the performance of other activities not necessarily of direct relevance to the customer. More information on this subject is contained in the CCTA Market Testing booklet Performance Measurement for IS/IT Services.

For the IT Services Organization, the relationship between objectives and planned activities is very complex:

* most activities contribute to several objectives

* most objectives depend on several activities from different functions.

The recommended approach is to base IT Services Organization planning on the functional areas described in section 3.0.2.

Objectives which are related to infrastructure improvement initiatives should be treated as discrete projects within the IT Services Organization.

As part of its planning to meet the purpose set by the business, the IT Services Management Team needs to derive its own:

* strategic plan

* tactical plans for

    - IT services provision

    - IT services infrastructure

* operational plans for managing its staff and controlling the use of its technical and financial resources.

The plans to be created in the IT Services Organization are described in Annex D, section D.3 and the process of creating these plans is discussed in section 4.1.5.

The operational plans are the basis upon which the managers in the IT Services Organization direct their resources. The plans are also used for monitoring the effect of their actions.

3.0.5 IT Services Organization control

Control consists of three activities; monitoring, reporting and taking corrective action. The IT Services Organization must collect information from within its own organization, act on this information, and report on its performance to managers outside IT Services Organization, so that they can control their own activities. That is, in order to fulfil its responsibilities, the IT Services Management Team must:

* monitor the status of the IT infrastructure, the progress of IT infrastructure improvement projects and the level of IT service provision

* identify divergences from the required levels of service and departures from plans

* take or initiate corrective action as appropriate, including changing plans if necessary

* report on the performance of the IT Services Organization to the IT Director and to relevant business managers and customers

* identify trends and make forecasts which may help prevent divergence from plans in the future.

Reporting mechanisms are described in more detail in section 4.1.3 and taking corrective action is discussed in 5.1.4.

3.1 Procedures

This section sets out the procedures for preparing for the implementation of a new or revised planning and control system in the IT Services Organization:

* determine the objectives and requirements for a planning and control system (3.1.1)

* conduct a review of current practice ensuring that procedures are documented (3.1.2)

* evaluate the effectiveness of current practice against the objectives; refine and agree the objectives (3.1.3)

* specify the new or modified planning and control system (3.1.4)

* plan and cost the introduction and operation of the new system (3.1.5)

* justify the change and obtain commitment (3.1.6)

* appoint a manager for the implementation of the new planning and control system (3.1.7).

3.1.1 Determine the objectives and requirements for a planning and control system

The principal aim of the IT Services Organization's planning and control system should be supporting the provision of IT services in accordance with the performance requirements of Service Level Agreements. This aim should form the basis of the objectives set down when implementing a planning and control system in the IT Services Organization. These objectives should subsequently form the basis for measuring and evaluating how successfully the planning and control system is in fulfilling its stated purpose.

It is recommended that these objectives are drawn up by a team led by the IT Services Manager, who will involve other managers as appropriate. This ensures effective and visible ownership of the results.

The team should review the available documentation to ensure that there is a complete understanding of the IT Services Organization's purpose as defined in 3.0.3. The team should have available:

* IT Services Organization mission

* plans and requirements relevant to IT service provision

* related policies, procedures, standards and guidelines.

3.1.2 Review the existing planning and control system

The review should involve the managers of the various IT Services Organization functions and should cover:

* the policy relating to planning

* the possible setting of benchmarks against which to measure improvement

* plans

* management reports

* documentation of procedures.

Policy

The review of the policy relating to the internal planning of the IT Services Organization should ensure that it is in line with that contained in the Corporate Policies and Procedures Manual.

Benchmarks

In order to measure the performance of the IT Services Organization following the introduction of a planning and control system, benchmarks need to be set against which future measurement of performance can be compared. The benchmarks to be set should be related to the objectives identified to justify implementation of the planning and control system.

Plans

The review of current IT services plans should check:

* if the plans refer to the current business and IS plans

* if they are adequate for their purpose

* if they are kept up-to-date and used as managerial tools

* if people are working in accordance with the plans

                 *   if estimates are

                     -   realistic

                     -   refined in the light of actual usage

                     -   used for financial or other resource budget control

                 *   how much effort is put into planning in the IT Services Organization.

Reports

The review of the IT Services Organization's management reports and project reports should cover:

* their relevance, adequacy, timeliness and consistency

* how the usage of human and technical resources is currently tracked and reported

* how much time and effort is currently put into the reporting process.

Documentation

The procedures associated with planning and control should be documented. If this has been done already, the documentation should be reviewed for accuracy and completeness. Any inaccuracies should be corrected and any gaps filled, so that the outcome of the review process is a documented IT Services planning and control system.

3.1.3 Evaluate the effectiveness of the current planning and control system

The evaluation of the current efficiency and effectiveness of planning and control for the IT Services Organization should:

* measure planning and control against the stated objectives

* include an estimate of the cost to the business of failures in the planning and control system.

Inadequate planning and control generally generates three types of problem for the IT Services Organization:

* delays in IT Services Organization's projects, for instance when upgrading the IT infrastructure, when inter-dependant activities are not coordinated

* bad estimating of demand for infrastructure resources

* shortcomings in the existing service provision caused by overloading.

The potential cost impacts of these failures include:

* lost revenue or additional cost to the business because of delays in putting services into operation

* the late availability of extra infrastructure resources

* unnecessary costs because of expenditure on the infrastructure too early.

3.1.4 Specify the planning and control system

The next step is to decide on the level of planning and control appropriate for the organization. The elements to be specified are:

* the local **policies and standards** to be adopted in the production of plans

* the **plans** needed and the procedures associated with their production (summarized in 3.0.4)

* the **controls** which must be applied and the reports needed to monitor achievement of plans.

Management reports should be:

* relevant and necessary to check delivery against a particular plan

* produced at the appropriate time, covering a period that is significant for monitoring that particular plan, so as to allow managerial action when necessary

* able to provide information to facilitate managerial control by being quantitative, objective, complete and in a consistent and clear format.

Further guidance on the plans, controls and reports required is contained in Annex D.

The allocation of responsibilities and level of staff needed to support planning and control need to be specified. The key roles of this support function are:

* coordinating (but not authorizing) the creation and development of plans and other supporting documentation in the IT Services Organization

* analyzing and consolidating reports generated by functions in the IT Services Organization in order to identify actual or predicted deviations from plans

* advising the IT Services Manager on planning aspects and on corrective action when deviations are identified

* maintaining a library of plans for reference.

Some of the issues concerning staffing are discussed in Annex C (section C.2) of this module. There is more discussion in the IT Infrastructure Library **IT Services Organization** module.

The planning and control organization, procedures and practices should be embedded into the IT Services Organization's QMS. See the IT Infrastructure module for more information.

3.1.5 Plan and cost the new planning and control system

Having specified the form of the new planning and control system, it is then necessary to:

* plan its introduction (as a project) (section 4)

* cost its introduction (section 6.2)

* cost its operation (section 6.2).

3.1.6 Justify and obtain commitment

The review of activities provides insight into the quality of current planning and control. To justify change, the business benefits of taking a planned approach must be set against the costs of implementation.

The justification for better planning and control should highlight:

* the benefits to the business of a planned approach to IT service provision (section 6.1)

  - the improved management opportunities that effective control can provide

  - the areas where most benefit would be achieved through planning and control

* what is required to introduce improvements in planning and control

  - who in the IT and customer organizations has the information necessary for planning purposes

  - what resources are required to create a planning and control infrastructure, ie planning team, accommodation, support systems and administrative assistance, including basic cost and time estimates

* the cost and risk of not introducing better planning and control

  - which problems were caused by the lack of good planning (ie where it was the root cause not the effect)

  - the specific areas where control is inadequate.

The IT Services Manager should use this information to obtain commitment from the IT Services Management Team and from higher management as necessary.

3.1.7 Appoint manager to implement

The final step of the first stage is to appoint a manager to implement the planning and control system. This can be the IT Services Manager (ITSM) or a manager appointed by the ITSM specifically for the task, possibly from among the function managers.

Ideally, once the planning and control system has been implemented successfully, the manager responsible for the implementation should move on to managing the new system as the Planning and Control Manager. This role is described in 3.3.3.

3.2 Dependencies

The main dependencies when preparing to implement an effective and efficient planning and control system are that:

* the parent organization has a clearly defined expectation of its IT services and has supplied adequate planning documentation (see 3.0.3)

* the IT Services Organization Management Team is committed to the process and is responsible for it

29

* there is participation and co-operation between the IT Services Organization and its customers

* business and IT managers are involved in the planning process.

The IT Directorate is primarily responsible for managing these dependencies.

3.3   People

3.3.1 People and teams in IT Services Organization planning

Planning and control in the IT Services Organization requires effective teamwork across all functions that make up IT service provision. Such teams need:

* good direction

* an understanding of the objectives

* well defined roles and responsibilities

* individual team members who understand their part in the process and have the opportunity to participate effectively.

There are two key teams involved in planning and control for the IT Services Organization. These are illustrated in figure 4. The teams are:

* the IT Services Management Team. This is led by the IT Services Manager who also determines its composition. It typically consists of the managers responsible for the main IT Service functions as identified in figure 3

* the IT Services Planning and Control Team. This consists of specialists who are responsible for, or have detailed knowledge of, any IT Services Organization function which produces a plan. This team is described in more detail in 3.3.4.

In all but the largest IT Services Organizations it may be appropriate for managers to represent their functions directly on the IT Services Planning and Control Team. In this case, the composition of both teams will be similar or even identical. However, the need for the logical distinction in their function and purpose remains.

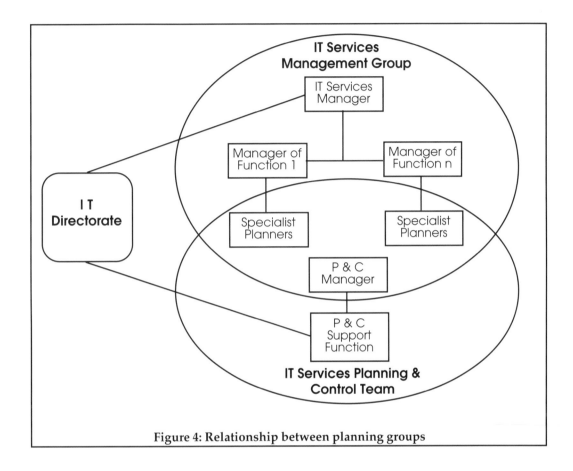

Figure 4: Relationship between planning groups

Both teams include the Planning and Control Manager whose role is described in 3.3.2 and 3.3.3. The Planning and Control Support function covers administrative roles described later in 3.3.5.

3.3.2 Key roles

There are two key roles involved in the preparation for the planning and control system:

*   the IT Services Manager who

    - is responsible for the provision of IT services within the organization and hence for planning and control

    - should manage the preparation for the introduction of a new planning and control system

* the IT Services Planning and Control Manager who

    - is appointed to implement the planning and control system

    - should ultimately coordinate the development of all IT Services Organization plans, document the procedures and monitor all reports (see 3.3.3).

In reality many organizations do not need nor have the resource to have a separate IT Services Planning and Control Manager, but will recognize the function that needs to be carried out and hence will identify the most suitable organizational structure.

3.3.3 IT Services Planning and Control Manager role

The role of the IT Services Planning and Control Manager is to:

* implement and monitor the IT Services Organization's planning and control system

* coordinate the production of the IT Services Organization's plans

* liaise with business, IS and programme planning teams, to ascertain impact on IT service provision

* manage the IT Services Planning and Control Team to produce, monitor and change the IT Services Organization's plans

* administer the documentation of procedures associated with the planning and control system

* manage the Planning and Control Support Unit, if it exists (see 3.3.5).

The IT Services Planning and Control Manager must have:

* good business understanding and perspective

* comprehensive IT experience

* awareness of planning and control issues

* sound management experience

* ability to manage the process of successfully introducing the changes arising from the new procedures (see 4.1.7). It may be appropriate to use specialist help or a dedicated resource in this role.

3.3.4 IT Services Planning and Control Team

This team, led by the IT Services Planning and Control Manager, consists of the staff responsible for planning and control in the IT Services Organization's functions.

Team members must:

* understand the technology which supports the services, including its capabilities and limitations

* be able to schedule resources effectively to match changing business requirements

* have good planning and control skills

* have a broad mix of analytical and inter-personal skills to understand the demands expressed by customers

* have a good understanding of the practical issues involved in providing and supporting IT.

3.3.5 Planning and control support

A full-time unit, the IT Services Planning and Control Support Unit, to support the Planning and Control function may be required in a large or rapidly changing IT Directorate. This unit is essentially administrative and is managed by the IT Services Planning and Control Manager.

When such a unit is set up, staff should be selected who have the following key qualities:

* understanding of IT planning process in general and relation to business planning

* understanding of IT services management

* ability to communicate with managers and the providers of reports

* familiarity with appropriate planning techniques and analytical and management tools (see section 7)

* familiarity with basic principles of cost management and management budgets and accounts.

As staff with these qualities are typically found in other support units which already exist in the IT Directorate, it may be convenient to combine a number of units.

Examples are:

* the Project Support Office (PSO)

* the IT Planning Unit (ITPU). The ITPU coordinates all planning activities within an IT Directorate, monitors achievements against plans and subsequently reviews the plans. The role of an ITPU is summarized in Annex C, section C.2.

Figure 5 shows the role of the IT Services Planning and Control Team within the overall IS Planning and Control function.

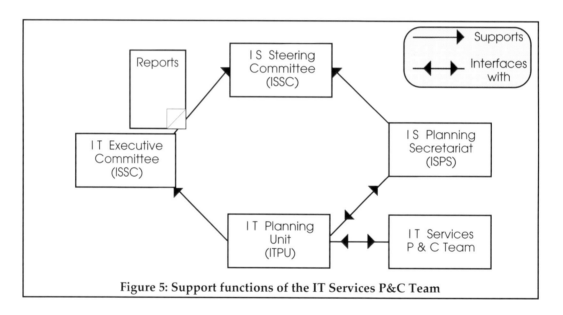

Figure 5: Support functions of the IT Services P&C Team

3.4   Timing

Planning and control is a key to long term improvements in the cost and quality of IT services. So if an IT Services Organization has not already implemented formal planning and control processes, it should consider doing so as soon as the dependencies described in section 3.2 can be satisfied - but ideally not before this has been done.

Planning and control is likely to evolve as part of setting up other IT service management functions eg Cost Management, Capacity Management. However, it is desirable to look at planning and control as a whole, which can be done at any time after some functions have been developed.

4. Implementation

This section gives guidance on how to develop and introduce the new planning and control system into the IT Services Organization. This is the next step after approval and commitment have been obtained. The section covers:

* the procedures (4.1)

* critical dependencies (4.2)

* the involvement of key people (4.3)

* the timing of the introduction (4.4).

4.1 Procedures

4.1.1 Introduction and summary

This section defines the main procedures which are normally required in order to implement a new or revised planning and control system into an IT Services Organization. The section should be used as a guide only; managers and planners will need to adapt it to meet the actual needs and circumstances of their own organization.

The implementation of a planning and control system should be treated as a project and divided into phases. This approach allows review points at the end of each phase when the IT Services Management Team can reconsider the implications of introducing the system and modify the approach if necessary.

The five phases are listed below and elaborated in later sections:

* initiating the project; establishing the project on a sound footing (4.1.2)

* establishing the control element of the planning and control system (4.1.3)

* collecting data and reviewing the planning and control (4.1.4)

* writing IT Services Organization plans (4.1.5)

* integrating the fully defined planning and control system into the organization's Quality Management System (4.1.6).

Managing the project should follow normal local practice.

The agreed approach should include:

* clear project organization and responsibilities

* procedures for reporting up the management chain as required on results, variances from plan and corrective action in hand.

Development of some of the phases may proceed in parallel. Management of these activities, as part of the management of change, is described in 4.1.7.

At the end of the five phases involved in implementation, monitoring of the operation of the planning and control system begins (see section 5).

4.1.2 Initiating the project

This phase sets the implementation project on a firm foundation. The main activities during this phase are the production of Quality Improvement Plans which:

* establish the project team with defined responsibilities and clear task directives

* establish and agree objectives for the planning and control system based on the justification and commitment obtained in the previous stage (3.1.6)

* agree milestones, success criteria and reporting requirements

* agree the management approach (4.1.7)

* produce and agree management plans showing resource requirements, dependencies and timescales for implementing the planning and control system

* initiate a programme of presentations to keep staff informed.

The manager of the project, referred to here as the Planning and Control Manager, should have been appointed at the end of the previous stage (3.1.7).

It is recommended that the project board is the IT Services Management Team (3.3.1) and the project team is the intended IT Services Planning and Control Team (3.3.4).

4.1.3 Establishing the control element of the planning and control system

Control depends on the reporting process producing good information, and taking appropriate action to achieve the desired objectives.

Setting up a control system involves defining and promulgating procedures for collecting and reporting the required data (control measures). The Planning and Control Team is the most appropriate group to define these procedures.

To manage the resources effectively the IT Services Management Team must receive reports on:

* the quality of service provided with comparisons against previous periods

* the performance of the IT infrastructure

  - how resources are currently utilized

  - the levels of growth expected

  - the capacity available for growth in each resource area

  - the business risk if the resource fails to meet expectations

  - how the risk is minimized

  - arrangements for corrective action to deal with major failures

* the costs associated with providing IT services

* staff utilization (time allocated to specific activities).

The reports commonly used in IT Services Organizations are illustrated in figure 6, overleaf, and summarized in the next two sections.

4.1.3.1 Customer and Management Reports

The most important management reports produced for customers by the IT Services Organization give details of performance against Service Level Agreements (SLAs) on a service-by-service basis.

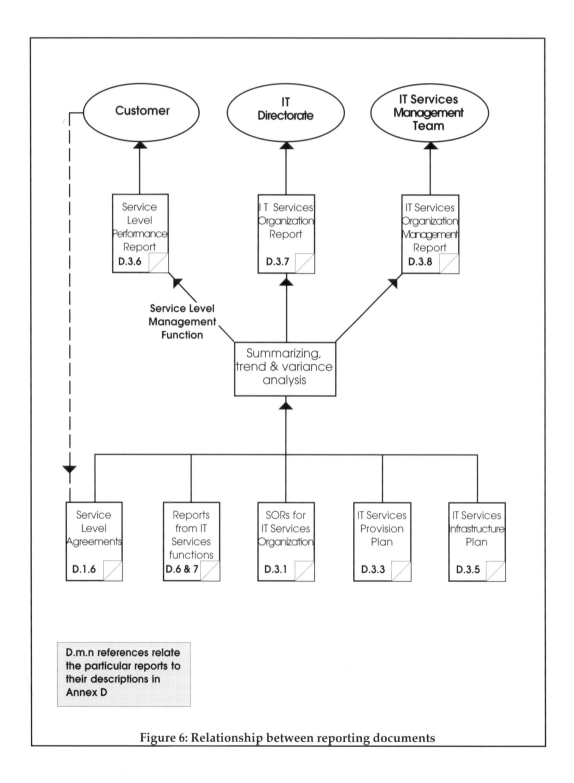

Figure 6: Relationship between reporting documents

Customers must be provided with regular reports on the quality of the IT services provided. This is normally done in terms of the level of the service provided compared to the targets set out in the Service Level Agreement (SLA).

The reasons for not meeting the SLA targets, and action taken or planned to prevent a recurrence, should always be provided whatever the cause of failure.

One particular type of management report, the IT Services Organization Report (D3.7), advises programme managers and IT project managers of activities within the IT Services Organization which affect their plans.

The IT Directorate must also be provided with a report summarizing performance against targets, particularly service level and financial, of the IT Services Organization.

The IT Services Management Report is considered by the Management Team who decide on corrective action. This is defined as a Request for Change and passed to the Change Management function for action. See the IT Infrastructure Library **Change Management** module.

The Customer and Management Reports are described in Annex D, section D.3.

4.1.3.2 Internal Reports

The IT Services Organization must also produce internal reports on the utilization of resources and on service performance. In addition, the IT Services Organization must also report on the performance of the technology, the support staff, and any external service providers.

In most cases the reports give details of the current position against plans (as defined in 4.1.5). However, plans may not be in place when the planning and control system is being set up. Even so, the reports can be produced and used for control and as an essential aid to writing the plans for the first time.

The key internal reports are defined in Annex D, sections D.6 and D.7. In most cases, the references given in the annex to IT Infrastructure Library modules will show where more information can be found.

The reports are:

* Customer Requests Assessment Report

* Problem and User Incident Report

* Customer Satisfaction Questionnaire

* Contingency Plan Audit Report

* Capacity Performance Report

* Security Status Report

* Security Audit Report

* Operations Performance Report

* Staff Report

* Financial Performance Report

* Change Management Report

* Quality Status Report

* Quality Audit Report

* Report on Performance of Supplier

* Supplier Rating

* Planning and Control Status Report.

The reports must be sent to the Planning and Control function for analysis and consolidation. This function can be tasked with generating the management reports described in the previous section. For convenience, some of the reports can be presented as appendices to the main body of the management report.

4.1.4 Collecting data and reviewing

When the control system has operated for a period, say a month, the collected data can be analyzed, and the results of the analysis used to review and amend the specification of the planning and control system to:

* revise the selection of controls and data collection procedures in the light of experience

* fully define the contents of each plan which must be produced, define who is responsible for writing it and how it is to be produced

* refine and fully specify the planning procedures, reporting and change control procedures and the Planning and Control Support function.

This is also an appropriate point at which to validate the costs of both implementation and operation of the planning and control system, update the justification and review with management.

4.1.5 Writing IT Services Organization plans

The plans defined during the previous phase (4.1.4) should be produced in accordance with the procedures which have already been established. Annex B, section B.4, describes the planning and control process in general. Writing the plans should be tied to the organization's planning cycle (normally, the financial year).

The relationship between the plans required is illustrated in figure 7, overleaf.

The planning activity takes place in four steps:

i   consolidate requirements into the Specification of Requirements for the IT Services Organization

ii   produce (or update) the IT Services Organization Strategic Plan(D.3.2)

iii   Produce the IT Services Provision Plan(D.3.3) on the basis of the consolidated requirements and the IT Services Organization Strategic Plan. This includes a number of separate plans which define the way IT services will be delivered by the IT Services Organization

- Capacity Plan

- Contingency Plan

- Customer Support Plan (including full details for service provision, support and development)

- Availability Plan

- Security Implementation and Audit Schedule

- Application Implementation Support Plan

  These plans are produced by the relevant function manager in the IT Services Organization

iv   Produce the IT Services Infrastructure Plan(D.3.5) by consolidating those function plans which relate to the infrastructure

- Configuration Plan (current status of the infrastructure)

- Change Plan (the main planned changes to the infrastructure)

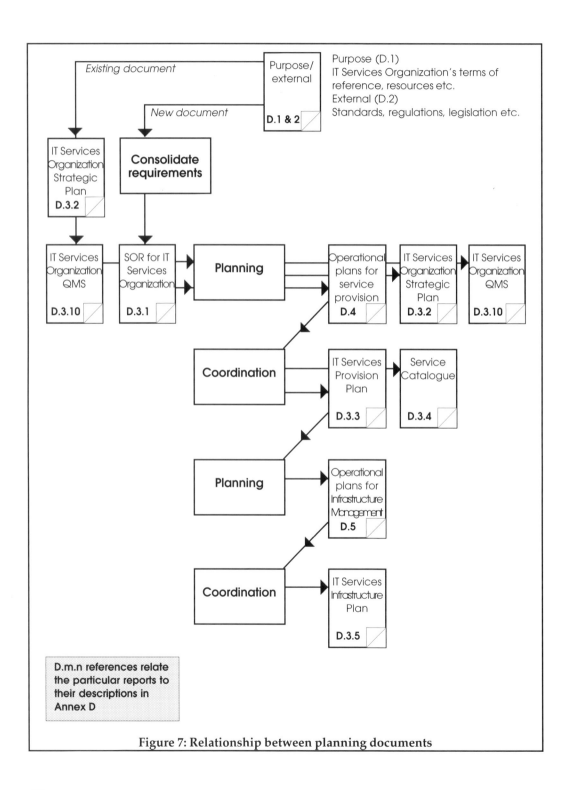

Figure 7: Relationship between planning documents

- Staff Plan (people involved in planning, management, implementation and operation of the IT and environmental infrastructure)

- Financial Plan (a full range of budgets and cash flow forecasts)

- Environmental Plan (accommodation plans for both the IT Services Organization and the technology operations areas)

- Operations Plan (plans for supporting and replacing software, and regular hardware maintenance)

- Quality Management System Amendment Plan and Audit Schedule

The Planning and Control function must consolidate these plans ensuring that they are consistent with the requirements, the strategy and each other. Discrepancies must be resolved by discussion either in the Planning and Control Team or the IT Services Management Team. The plans are then consolidated as the IT Services Infrastructure Plan.

4.1.6 Integrating into the Quality Management System

The procedures and the definition of the planning and control system should be integrated into the organization's Quality Management System if one exists. In any case, once written and established, the definition of the planning and control system must be subject to review and change control using the organization's normal procedures.

4.1.7 Management of change

The introduction of formal planning and control is likely to be a significant change for the IT Services Organization. Managing this change effectively is a critical responsibility which has two main aspects:

* management of change in the organization's culture and processes, ie what it does and how it does it

* management of the project as a set of activities.

Resistance to change is a natural human characteristic. Overcoming this resistance needs sensitivity and forethought. The advice of specialists in the management of change may be helpful.

The effort required to ensure this change is achieved will depend on the degree of change and size of the organization but it is often significant. Economizing on this area is likely to compromise the full benefit of the new system. The key player in this process is the IT Services Planning and Control Manager(3.3.3).

Change in culture and processes

The new planning and control procedures will affect customers, suppliers and IT Services managers and staff. Each group of people concerned must be prepared for the new way of working, so that they:

* understand the value of the new planning and control system, and how it contributes to the IT Services Organization's success

* are committed to making it successful

* know what is expected of them and when their co-operation is needed.

To sustain this commitment and co-operation, it is necessary to ensure that there is ongoing communication about:

* progress towards attainment of project objectives

* changed procedures through adequate and timely training where necessary.

4.2 Dependencies

There are four key dependencies for the successful introduction of a planning and control system whether it is an entirely new system, or a revised one. The dependencies are:

* the commitment of managers and staff

* a business case for formal planning and control endorsed by management

* clear requirements for the IT Services Organization's purpose

* adequate resources to introduce and operate the new system.

Commitment

It is essential that the IT Directorate, and the IT Services Management Team, supports the IT Services Organization planning and control project and obtains the support of customers, suppliers and IT Services Organization staff.

Business case

Given that resources are finite, the business must balance the benefits of improving the planning and control process for the IT Services Organization against the benefits of allocating the resource to other projects. The IT Directorate must ensure that the business reaches the decision to support the IT Services Organization planning and control project before embarking upon it (see 3.1.6).

Purpose

The IT Services Organization must have a clear understanding of its purpose. This is expressed in documents including mission statement, terms of reference, business plans, IS strategy, infrastructure project plans and customer requirements. These are described in section D.1, and should be available from customers and senior management.

Resources

Adequate and suitable resources are required for effective planning and control, and it is essential that they are available from the start of the project.

Effective implementation of a planning and control system for a large IT Directorate may need some form of administrative support function. If so, this should be established by the IT Services Planning and Control Manager before embarking on the implementation project.

The members of the IT Services Planning and Control Team involved in the project must be adequately trained (see 3.3.4 for needs).

The resources required are:

* accommodation

* software tools and the hardware necessary to run them

* adequate administrative and clerical support for data and document management.

4.3 People

4.3.1 People involved in implementation

The implementation of a planning and control system will affect several groups of people:

* customers

* business managers

* staff in the IT Services Organization

* IT Directorate management

* IT Services Management Team

* IT Services Planning and Control Manager (see 3.3.3)

* IT Services Planning and Control Team (see 3.3.4)

* IT Services Planning and Control Support Unit (see 3.3.5.).

All these groups will have to be considered as part of the management of change (4.1.7).

4.4   Timing

The IT Services Organization's planning cycle should be aligned with the parent organization's budget cycle. For example, in government departments the Public Expenditure Survey(PES) cycle would be appropriate. This enables the IT Services Management Team to produce budgets for its staff and technical resources which are justified by business needs.

Ideally, implementation should not be hurried. It can take up to a year just to get all the controls in place and working effectively. But the drivers to implementing planning and control, see section 1, will almost certainly require that a pragmatic approach to its implementation be adopted. The completion of this phase should be timed, where possible, to allow the construction of the IT Services Organization's plans to fit in to the next planning period.

When developing plans it is advisable to follow the order suggested in 4.1.5.

5. Post-implementation and audit

This section covers the activities which follow the establishment of a planning and control system:

* * procedures

    - operating the Planning and Control function: planning (5.1.1); reporting (5.1.2); analyzing trends and forecasting (5.1.3); taking corrective action (5.1.4)

    - monitoring the effectiveness of planning and control (5.1.5)

    - controlling the quality of plans and reports (5.1.6)

    - auditing the planning and control system (5.1.7)

    - reviewing the project (5.1.8).

* * dependencies (5.2)

* * people involved (5.3)

* * timing (5.4).

5.1 Procedures

5.1.1 Planning

The planning process has been described in earlier sections (see 3.0.4 and 4.1.5). Repetitions of the planning process after the first time are generally much easier because of the availability of existing plans (from the previous cycle) and familiarity with the process.

5.1.2 Reporting

The reporting process has been described in earlier sections (see 3.0.5 and 4.1.3).

5.1.3 Analyzing trends and forecasting

Trend analysis and forecasting techniques are potentially of great value in planning and control of IT services. By maintaining an historical record of selected parameters, trends can be identified which may be used to improve forecasts. Experience, judgment and other knowledge must be applied as well.

For example, if a trend of rising utilization of a particular IT service appears, it can easily be checked with the customer who may give a good business reason why this occurred and suggest whether or not the trend will reverse shortly.

The accuracy of forecasting can be improved by comparing previous trend values and forecasts with actual performance. This will show if enough accurate data is being collected, and allow the manager to check the assumptions made in arriving at a forecast. This is especially important if an automated tool is being used (a spreadsheet, a standard calculation, or simulation, for example). Blind belief in the results of such tools is unwise.

5.1.4 Taking corrective action

Forecasting is done in order that managers may alter the course of events. "What if" forecasting helps them reach the right decision. That is, a prediction is made on the basis of current facts and corrective action must be taken if the prediction is not in line with the goals laid down in the plans. Note that the plans are always changed because either or both of the following reasons apply:

* the goals are modified

* resources are applied in a different way - more resources, different resources, new priorities, or modified procedures for instance.

5.1.5 Monitoring the effectiveness of planning and control

Metrics to assess the effectiveness of the Planning and Control function must be defined and monitored on a regular basis, as appropriate. The collection, interpretation and presentation of these metrics should be carried out in a formally defined way to ensure that results are consistent.

The following are typical examples of metrics for the efficiency and effectiveness of planning and control:

* number of corrective actions initiated by the Planning and Control function

* number of unplanned changes and the level of resource used to handle these changes

* accuracy of resource estimates and budget allocation against actual use

* actual cost of operating the IT Services Organization compared with budgeted cost

* number of changes to a plan (this could indicate responsiveness to change or inaccuracy in estimates and the metrics must differentiate between them)

* amount and frequency of resource rescheduling

* number of unanticipated follow-on projects and activities

* delay in completing projects due to resource conflict within the IT Services Organization

* accuracy of trends and forecasts.

Support staff can collect the information needed for these metrics, but the experience and judgement of the Planning and Control Manager is essential for interpreting them.

Unplanned activities may be due to poor planning in the IT Services Organization, but they may also be caused by inadequate warning from customers. In the latter case, the IT Services Management Team should still take the responsibility for improving the service jointly with the customer.

5.1.6 Carrying out quality control reviews

Quality control reviews examine the products of planning and control (the plans, reports and corrective actions) to see how well they meet the needs of the organization.

The Planning and Control Manager should check plans as they are submitted for alignment with the business and IS plans. In particular, it must be possible to identify the business objectives supported by each IT service.

Management reports should be checked for their relevance, completeness, accuracy, consistency and timeliness.

An inadequate plan or report may reflect poor procedures rather than poor preparation of the plan or report. Procedures must therefore be reviewed as well as the plans and reports. The next section describes the way in which inadequate procedures are detected and improved.

5.1.7 Auditing the system

The planning and control system must be an effective management tool, so it is important to review its efficiency and effectiveness regularly. This will ensure that the function continues to contribute to the objectives of the IT Services Organization and hence to the objectives of its parent organization. The reviews should be carried out in line with the organization's Quality Management System(QMS).

The audit should be carried out annually by an independent team which can be:

* an internal team of specialist auditors

* non-specialist staff drawn from within the organization for each audit

* external consultants.

The audit is designed to see how well the documented procedures are being followed and whether they are effective. This is achieved by:

* examining plans and reports for conformance to required format and content

* checking that plans reflect the current situation and actual management intentions

* checking that procedures for reporting, trend analysis and corrective action are being followed

* checking that there is an audit trail associated with corrective action and changes to plans.

See the IT Infrastructure Library module, **Quality Management for IT Services**, for more information.

5.1.8 Reviewing the planning and control implementation project

Project reviews should be carried out when the Planning and Control function has been implemented as a formal project. These reviews report on the success of:

* the project itself, for instance, against timescales and resources allocated

* the changes introduced eg meeting improvement objectives set following implementation of the Planning and Control function.

There are two types of review:

* a Project Evaluation Review (PER) which assesses the project that implemented the new or revised Planning and Control function. The review report should identify

  - whether planned targets, critical success factors and objectives of the project were achieved

  - any lessons to be learned

* a Post-Implementation Review (PIR) which provides a means of assessing whether the new or revised function has successfully realized the objectives and achieved the targets set for it. A PIR should be carried out six months to a year after completion of the project, to assess, for example, whether

  - planning and control in the IT Services Organization has improved service to customers

  - cost, time and functionality targets are being met, or even exceeded.

5.2 Dependencies

A key dependency is an adequately staffed Planning and Control function. Other key dependencies are those already identified in 4.2.

5.3 People

Most staff in the IT Services Organization are involved with the operation of the IT services planning and control system:

* collecting and reporting the data

* constructing and maintaining the plans (the Planning and Control Team)

* authorising the plans (the IT Services Management Team)

* analyzing the data and collating plans (the IT Services Planning and Control Support Unit)

* auditing the planning and control system.

See 3.3 for details of the people, their skills and capabilities, who carry out these roles and tasks. Other review roles are described in sections 5.1.6 - 5.1.8.

5.4   Timing

A Project Evaluation Review can be carried out as soon as the project to implement planning and control has been completed. A Post-Implementation Review should only be carried out when sufficient information is available on the impact on the organization of the changes to the planning and control system.

Audits of the planning and control system should be carried out three months after it is established and then annually. The IT Services Management Team may also require an audit of all or part of the procedures following a serious failure to deliver the required level of service.

6. Benefits, costs and possible problems

This section covers:

* the benefits of a planning and control system (6.1)

* the costs of such a system (6.2)

* the problems which may be encountered when introducing the system (6.3).

All the benefits from a well planned and controlled approach to IT service provision contribute to the overall quality of service. Some result directly in cost savings which offset the costs of introducing and running a planning and control system.

6.1 Benefits

6.1.1 For customers

Customers should see that the IT Services Organization can deliver the required level of services better, and respond to new requirements more effectively. The main factors producing benefits for customers are:

* The IT Services Organization's plans are formally derived from their own Statements of Service Requirements, and resultant Service Level Agreements so that

  - services match business needs

  - problems are overcome more appropriately because there is better understanding of business needs and priorities

  - better solutions to resourcing conflicts are adopted because consequences of service failures are appreciated in the IT Services Organization

  - cost effective resilience, and resistance to accidental interruption or deliberate interference can be built into operational processes

  - the vulnerabilities and threats associated with the continuity and reliability of each IT service can be clearly defined on the basis of sound information so that the counter-measures can be cost effectively designed to meet business priorities

* there are fewer failures of service and unplanned variations in service, and better warning of any unavoidable problems

* customers' changing requirements are anticipated and resourced more accurately

* customers are kept informed about actual performance, costs etc through reports.

6.1.2 For the parent organization

The main benefits to the parent organization are:

* greater efficiency and effectiveness through more informed planning of future requirements for IT service provision

* reduction of costs through

 - better matching of resources to need

 - less waste from delays and idle resources

 - lower charges from suppliers (6.1.3)

* documented information about resource usage and achievement of objectives (reports).

6.1.3 For suppliers

The main benefits to suppliers are that they can provide a better service more efficiently because they are better informed about the IT Services Organization's needs. This enhances the quality of IT services.

In this context the Applications Development Group may be regarded as a supplier. Improved efficiency may be reflected indirectly in lower costs to the parent organization.

6.1.4 For the IT Services Management Team

The main benefits for the IT Services Management Team are:

* the availability of reliable, timely, accurate and pertinent information which increases managers' awareness of the events and trends which might impact upon IT service provision. This

 - improves the effectiveness of preventative activities, including contingency planning, so increasing control over events

- enables managers to identify and resolve the causes of problems rather than just treat the symptoms

- supports trend analysis thereby aiding the continuous improvement of management effectiveness and efficiency

* more management time is released for prevention as less time is spent having to react to events

* "what if" predictions can be made based on plans and the use of resource management and scheduling techniques

* technical and staff resources can be directed, allocated and prioritized more effectively

* new demands, unexpected events, or other day-to-day problems can be responded to more effectively, since the allocation of resources and priorities is known.

6.1.5 For IT Services Organization staff

The main benefit for IT staff is that all members of the organization can identify with the rewards from the success achieved in providing improved service at reduced cost, and participate in those improvements.

6.2 Costs

The organization will incur initial investment costs when formal planning and control methods are introduced. These costs will be for:

* training of staff in the tools and techniques necessary to be able to plan effectively

* support tools required for both planning, and planning support functions

* staff, who may need to be recruited or redeployed into the Planning and Control function, particularly the Planning and Control Support Unit, if it is decided such a dedicated unit is appropriate. This will eventually increase staff productivity.

There will also be ongoing expenditure associated with running a Planning and Control function including staffing and accommodation costs. However, these costs will be offset by the benefits outlined in 6.1.

6.3 Possible problems

The main problems when formal planning and control is introduced in the IT Services Organization are likely to be related to customer and IT staff acceptance of new working practices. The pace of the implementation of formal planning and control will be dictated by the degree of change required and the cultural resistance to change.

The basic reason for resistance is usually the normal human distrust of any change. Overcoming this distrust requires sensitivity and the ability to convince people who will advance apparently logical reasons to justify their resistance.

Other potential problems are:

* IT Services Organization planning may be held up by the lack of direction from business planning and IS strategic planning

* the information needed for introducing formal planning may not exist within the organization

* the process of planning may take over from the actual tasks required (the IT Services Management Team must monitor the effort involved in following the planning and control procedures and ensure it remains within the expected limits)

* the implementation of a planned approach to IT service delivery and support may be seen as reducing the IT Services Organization's ability to respond. This can lead to resistance, which is most effectively countered when the IT Services Organization consistently delivers the services it is committed to supply.

7. Tools

No tools have been identified which are specifically for IT Services Organization planning and control. General purpose project management software tools, of which there are many, can be used to document plans and track progress. However, they do not provide the range and levels of functionality that are necessary to fully support the IT service activities.

Spreadsheets, databases, word processing and graphics packages are also useful for data collection, manipulation and presentation for planning, resource tracking and management reporting purposes.

It is important that all tools provide a good quality graphic presentation of plans, procedures and reports to maximize the information content but minimize the amount of data presented.

Four specific categories of tools are described in the following sections for:

* estimating (7.1)

* resource management (7.2)

* management reporting (7.3)

* strategic planning (7.4).

7.1 Estimating tools

There are no specific estimating tools available at present for IT Services Organizations. The best approach is to tabulate the work breakdown on a spreadsheet. As each task is completed, the actual time and resources required can be recorded and compared with the estimate and a rolling forecast be maintained.

7.2 Resource management tools

An on-going plan of current and expected commitments and availability must be maintained for each human and technical resource. Some spreadsheet and graphics packages are available that provide sufficient customization ability to be useful in maintaining such plans.

7.3 Management reporting tools

The main aspects involved in management reporting are the:

* collection of management data

* consolidation and analysis of the data

* reporting and presentation of the information.

Collection of data

This is the most difficult management reporting task to define and implement. Tools, such as database management systems, can be helpful for this task. Ideally, much of the management information required should be available from existing information systems. In practice, this is often not the case and the core systems need to be modified to collect and present this data. Alternatively, rule based data collection tools can be used to select the data.

Consolidation and analysis

This is mainly a data design exercise. If the analysis and consolidation requirements are specified before the detail of the data collection requirements are specified, then the collected data will be in a format that simplifies the analysis and consolidation process.

The consolidation, analysis, and presentation aspects can competently be carried out by linked spreadsheet and graphics packages. These will satisfy most managers' requirements. More sophisticated analysis can be achieved by the use of statistical analysis and reporting packages.

7.4 Strategic planning tools

There are few strategic planning tools available which could be used for IT Services Organization planning. Of those that are available, many are part of a specific proprietary planning method. Detailed knowledge of the method is normally a prerequisite for using the tool successfully.

Some information management software packages can provide some of the basic functionality required for a strategic study. However, the capabilities of these packages are limited and do not provide the types of matrix reporting and printing functions that are often required.

8. Bibliography

8.1 CCTA publications

Information Systems Engineering Library
SSADM and Capacity Planning
Published by HMSO
ISBN 0 11 330577 X

Information Systems Guide A2
Strategic Planning for Information Systems
Published by John Wiley & Sons, Chichester 1989
ISBN 0 471 92522 5

IS Planning Subject Guide
The Role of the IT Planning Unit
Published by CCTA, 1991
ISBN 0 946683 41 7

IT Infrastructure Library
Published by HMSO.

Market Testing IS/IT
Performance Measurement for IS/IT Services
Published by CCTA
ISBN 0 946683 66 2

An Introduction to Programme Management
ISBN 0 11 330611 3

A Guide to Programme Management
ISBN 0 11 330612 1

An Introduction to Infrastructure Planning

PRINCE Manuals
Published by NCC Blackwell Ltd, Oxford 1990

PRINCE Practitioner Handbooks
Published by HMSO

Quality Management Library
Published by HMSO, 1992
ISBN 0 11 330569 9

8.2 Standards

ISO 9000 series references

Published in the UK by the British Standards Institution

8.3   General

Information Systems Management in Practice
Sprague, Ralph H; McNurlin, Barbara C
Published by Prentice-Hall, London 1986
ISBN 0 13 464934 6

Information Systems Planning
Peterson, R O
Published by McGraw-Hill, Maidenhead 1990
ISBN 0 07 049649 8

Information Systems Strategic Planning:
A Source of Competitive Advantage
Andreu, R; Ricart, J E; Valor, J
Published by NCC Blackwell, Oxford 1991
ISBN 1 85554 140 8

Planning and Design of Information Systems
Blokdijk, A; Blokdijk, P
Published by Academic Press, London 1987
ISBN 0 12 107070 0

Planning for Effective Business Information Systems
Tozer, Edwin E
Published by Pergamon Press, Oxford 1988
ISBN 0 08 033359 1

Planning for Information as a Corporate Resource
(edited by) Collins, A
Published by Pergamon Press

Strategic Information Systems
Development, Implementation, Case Studies
Remenyi, DSJ
Published by NCC Blackwell, Oxford 1990
ISBN 0 85012 757 2

Strategic Planning for Information Systems
Ward, John; Griffiths, Pat; Whitmore, Paul
Published by John Wiley & Sons, Chichester 1990
ISBN 0 471 92002 9

Strategic Service Management
(edited by) Boyle, D
Published by Pergamon Press
ISBN 0 08 037752-1

Annex A. Glossary of terms

Acronyms used in this module

CAB	Change Advisory Board
CRAMM	CCTA Risk Analysis and Management Methodology
IS	Information System
ISPS	Information Systems Planning Secretariat
ISSC	Information Systems Steering Committee
IT	Information Technology
ITEC	Information Technology Executive Committee
ITPU	Information Technology Planning Unit
PER	Project Evaluation Review
PES	Public Expenditure Survey
PIR	Post-Implementation Review
PRINCE	Projects In Controlled Environments
PSO	Project Support Office
QMS	Quality Management System
SCT	Service Control Team
SLA	Service Level Agreement
SSADM	Structured Systems Analysis and Design Method

Definitions of terms used and not explicitly described in this module

Application System	A combination of software and hardware which performs a specified business function.
Business Manager	Any manager in the IT Services Organization's customer or parent organization who is responsible for a business function or unit.
Customer	An organizational unit which uses IT services.
Help Desk	The Help Desk is the single point of contact between the IT Services Organization and customers, or their representatives, on a day-to-day basis.

IT Director	The manager responsible for the IT Directorate.
IT Directorate	The organizational unit which delivers IT services.
IT Planning Unit	A function of the IT Directorate reporting to the appropriate Executive Committee. The IT Planning Unit coordinates the planning activities of the IT Directorate.
PRINCE	The method adopted within government for planning, managing and controlling IS projects. It provides guidance on the management components (organization, plans and controls) and on the technical components (end products and the activities needed to produce them).
Programme Director	The senior business manager responsible for establishing, managing and completing a business programme.

Annex B. Planning and control concepts

B.1   Purpose and structure of this annex

This annex describes the basic concepts of planning and control in an organization. This annex does not address more general management issues, nor does it give guidance on directing resources or describe specific management techniques. There is a wealth of guidance available on these topics (see bibliography in section 8).

Contents of the annex are:

* the fundamental concepts of planning and control (B.2)

    - an introduction to the key factors and management activities

    - planning and control hierarchies and planning horizons

* factors which affect planning and control (B.3)

    - having the basic information on the purpose of the enterprise

    - knowing the current situation of the environment in which the enterprise works and the resources at the manager's disposal

* the planning and control process (B.4)

    - translating the information into a course of action (planning)

    - measuring the effects of executing the plan, comparing with the predictions in the plan and modifying the course of action accordingly (control)

    - reviewing the effects of execution, which may result in modification of the plan and even, in extreme cases, requesting additional resources or seeking a modification to the given goals and objectives

    - reporting on achievements and failures

* further discussion on the nature of strategic, tactical and operational planning in general (B.5, B.6 and B.7 respectively)

* business planning (B.8)

* the relationship of planning and control to a Quality Management System (B.9).

Information on the specifics of IS planning, including IT infrastructure planning is contained in Annex C.

B.2 Fundamental concepts of planning and control

B.2.1 Introduction

The successful management of a project or a department, or any enterprise, depends on several key factors:

* knowing what has to be achieved (the purpose)

* knowing what resources are available to achieve the purpose

* knowing how achievement is to be measured and what reports are needed

* directing the resources to achieve the purpose.

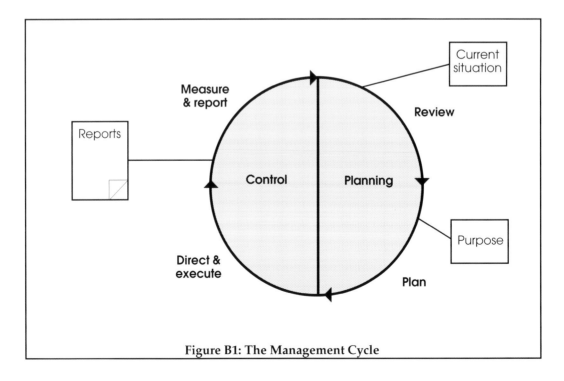

Figure B1: The Management Cycle

The management processes which are needed to achieve the purpose form a cycle, shown in figure B1, of:

* planning the activities which will meet the purpose

* directing the activities which execute the plan

* measuring the results of the execution of the plan

* reviewing the achievement against the plans and hence modifying the plans where necessary.

This cycle applies to two apparently different situations:

* project-type activities, which have a clearly defined beginning and end and well defined deliverables. There is a wealth of guidance on the management of such activities

* continuous activities, generally involving the management of resources. Guidance is more scarce on these situations.

IT services provision is a continuous activity, but with project-like elements. For example, it is likely to involve separate projects for the installation of a new component of the IT infrastructure or the preparation of a new IT service.

Planning relies on knowing purpose and current situation. For anything other than the initial planning exercise, the review of achievement against current plans will also be available.

Staff under the manager's direction carry out a plan, possibly organized in teams. The directions which these teams receive are their purpose and each team must conduct its own planning and control cycle.

Control involves measuring achievement and reporting. Reports are used within the management cycle to compare with plans and hence to take corrective action where necessary. Reports are also used to inform higher management, usually the same management team which issued the purpose.

B.2.2 Planning and control hierarchies

Planning and control occurs throughout an organization, from the most senior management board, which defines business direction, down to the lowest organizational unit, which has its own detailed business plan.

These business plans fall into three hierarchies of more detailed plans:

* plans, such as change programmes, which involve several organizational units

* plans which are confined to the activities within a single organizational unit

* plans for key topic areas, such as quality or security, and IS services, which are cross-business and cross-functional.

Ensuring that these plans are all consistent is a complex task, and recognizing the interdependencies is normally left to the good sense of individual managers. However, some organizations have found it appropriate to set up a planning department to coordinate the plans. For example, in the field of IS, CCTA recommends a number of coordinating committees supported by planning units. Annex C summarizes the recommendations.

The plans can also be divided into a time-related hierarchy generally designated strategic (long-term), tactical (medium-term) and operational (short-term). This hierarchy can apply to the set of business change programmes, to the functional plans and to the topic plans. This relationship is shown in figure B2, opposite.

For IT service delivery, the relevant plans would be:

* business strategy

* business change programmes

* the business function operational plans of the customers for IT services (as documented in Statements of Service Requirements)

* IS Strategy

* IS change programmes which deliver new IS (and which require IT infrastructure projects)

* IT infrastructure project plans (which are linked to business change and IS change programmes)

* Strategic Plan for the IT Services Organization

* IT Services Organization's tactical plans (the IT Service Provision Plan and the IT Services Organization's Infrastructure Plan)

* A range of operational plans which support the provision of IT services (eg availability plan, capacity plan, configuration plan).

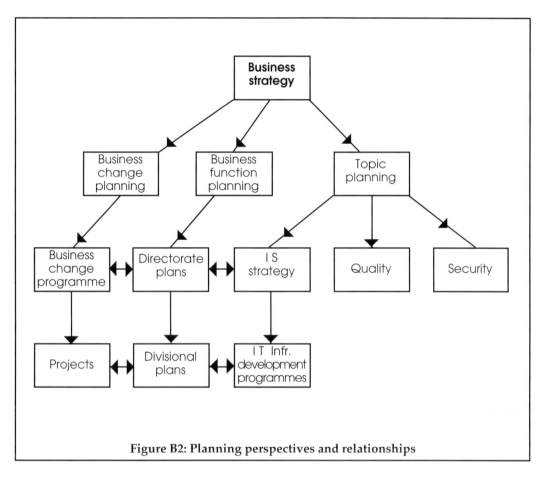

Figure B2: Planning perspectives and relationships

B.3 Factors that affect planning and control

B.3.1 General

The planning and control process is dependent on knowing purpose and current situation. This section considers these aspects in more detail.

Purpose consists of the following elements:

* mission and objectives or milestones (B.3.2)

* plans and specifications of requirements (B.3.3)

* policies, procedures, standards and guidelines relating to the manner in which the purpose is to be achieved (B.3.4).

Current situation consists of:

* the relevant environment (eg capability of suppliers' products for an implementation project or the market state for a business) (B.3.5)

* the resources available to achieve the purpose (eg staff, infrastructure, money) (B.3.5).

B.3.2 Mission and objectives

A mission is a succinct statement of what is to be achieved. It relates to the environment in which the organization operates. So it depends on the nature of the organization's business. An organization's highest level mission is translated into a hierarchy of missions corresponding to the organizational structure.

It is generally necessary to expand/extend the simple mission by listing a set of objectives with specific timeframes and measures. A project typically has a defined end-point and a department is normally assumed to exist beyond the timeframe being considered. In both cases, the definition of purpose must specify the timeframe and usually this will include interim milestones.

The following is an example for an IT Directorate.

Mission:	Provide comprehensive IT services which meet the company's business needs in the most cost effective way.
Objectives:	1 Meet existing commitments in 1994
	2 Bring new mainframe into service in April 1994
	3 Reduce staff levels by 20% by July 1994
	4 Develop new IT service to support cash management in the Accounts Dept by July 1995
	5 Prepare for certification to ISO 9001 by end 1995.

B.3.3 Plans and requirements

Plans and specifications of requirements are generally needed to fully define what is to be done. For instance, in the example above, objective 4 would have a set of plans

defining a business programme which included the
introduction of the new IT service. It would also refer to a
specification of the new service defining its function and
required performance.

**B.3.4 Policies, procedures,
        standards and
        guidelines**

Policies, procedures, standards and guidelines define and
constrain the manner in which a task is to be performed.

Policies

Policies are directions based on the stated principles and
objectives of the organization. Typical policy statements
which affect IT services are:

* service quality policy (eg ISO9001 certification)

* recruitment policy

* staff development and training policy

* procurement.

Procedures

Many of the routine activities within an organization must
follow defined procedures to enforce consistency. The
development of these procedures is influenced by policy
statements and the procedures frequently refer to standards
and guidelines.

Standards

Standards enforce compatibility across functional and
business boundaries. Standards may be specially written for
the organization or may be publicly available and generally
applicable.

Guidelines

Guidelines provide advice on how activities should be
performed. As with standards, they may be internal to a
business or an organizational unit or may be drawn from
outside the business.

B.3.5 Current situation

The manager needs to know about the current situation in
order to achieve the purpose. The current situation
includes:

* status of the external environment (business
  situation, customer and competitor trends, political,
  economic, social and technological trends)

* status of the resources available (human, financial,
  technical, etc).

The IT Infrastructure Library
Planning and Control for IT Services

In the initial planning stage, it is also important to forecast how the situation will change. Both external events and execution of the task will affect the situation, so forecasting requires good understanding of the processes involved.

As the plan is executed, the situation must be monitored, and a critical decision when the first version of a plan is formulated is to determine the factors which will be measured as part of this monitoring. These factors are discussed further in B.4.5.

B.4 Tasks within the planning and control process

The nature of planning and control was introduced in section B.2. This section expands on the activities involved in the planning and control process.

The planning and control process (illustrated in figure B3) consists of the following tasks:

* task assessment (B.4.1), consisting of

  - assess task requirements

  - define task to be performed

  - define local policies, procedures, standards and guidelines

* define subsidiary goals (B.4.2)

* create and modify plans (B.4.3)

* direct execution (B.4.4)

* monitor results of execution (B.4.5)

* compare results with plans (B.4.6)

* decide on corrective action (involving modification of plans or subsidiary goals or requesting relaxation of purpose by management) (B.4.7)

* report on achievements against plan, forecasts and corrective action in hand (B.4.8).

B.4.1 Task assessment

The task assessment activity must ensure that there is an effective system for planning and control. The given purpose should be reviewed, and if necessary clarification should be obtained, so that it is fully understood. This review can be used to produce a local definition or summary of the task if appropriate.

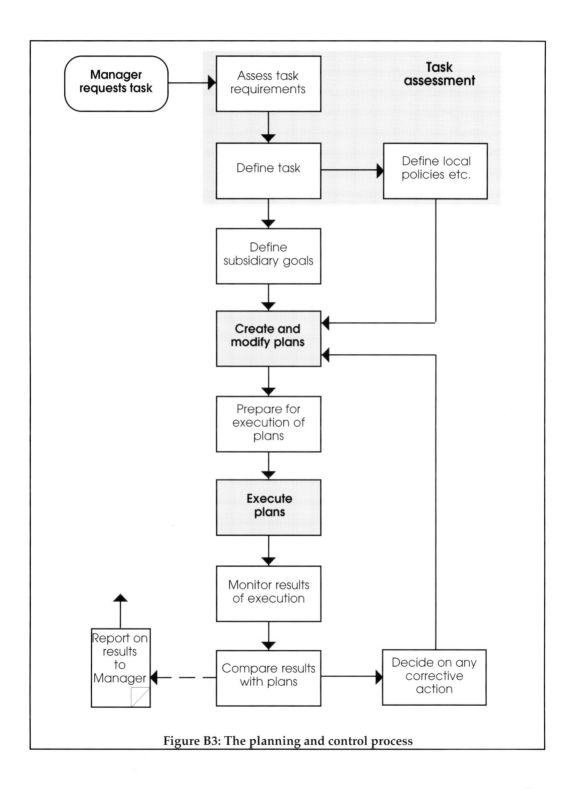

Figure B3: The planning and control process

It is also important to define the policies, procedures, standards and guidelines which must be applied to the task. Generally this definition will be by reference to those given as part of the purpose, but in many cases there are local procedures and standards which apply at a more detailed level.

The relationship of the planning and control system and the organization's Quality Management System is described further in section B.9.

B.4.2 Define subsidiary goals

Before creating a plan, it is often helpful to identify subsidiary goals first in order to plan for each of these separately. There are two main ways of doing this:

* break the purpose into phases, so a functional plan for the next year might be divided into quarters, and in a plan for a project, phases are likely to be linked to key deliverables

* break the purpose into distinct functional areas. For instance, IT service management breaks into IT service provision and IT infrastructure management.

B.4.3 Create and modify plans

A plan consists of:

* the purpose of the plan, its subsidiary goals, milestones and criteria for successful completion

* a definition of the status of the current situation (environment and resources)

* a list of assumptions

* a list of activities to be performed in order to achieve the goals of the plan

* the interdependencies between activities

* a timescale for the activities

* a definition of the resources required for the activities (including equipment, software, services and staff)

* a description of the relevant organizational structure and reports needed

* a definition of the financial impact of the plan (costs)

* a definition of any relevant measures of performance.

Plans can be created or modified in steps. Plan modification is similar to creation but normally confined to a particular area of the plan. Care must be taken to follow through the consequences of any potential change to check for unwanted effects.

Step 1

Subdivide the subsidiary goals defined during task assessment by:

* time (into sub-phases)

* function

* a combination of time and function.

During project planning, this subdivision is called Work Breakdown Structure (WBS), the lowest level elements are called activities, tasks or work packets. Other terms are used for other management environments. In managing cashflow, for instance, the breakdown would probably be on the basis of the calendar into months, weeks and days.

Step 2

Estimate the resources being planned. For a project, the resources needed to complete each task over a given period must be estimated. For a cashflow plan the estimates would be of the supply and demand in the period and a calculation of the forecast final balance.

Step 3

Define measures - A critical part of the plan creation process is defining the measures for assessing the achievement of the purpose. Managers should set thresholds on measures, which will indicate that corrective action must be taken if the thresholds are reached. These should be decided during the planning stage and adjusted in the light of experience. Measures are discussed in section B.4.5 and corrective action in B.4.7.

Risk assessment is a critical part of planning. The objective is to assess and quantify the potential areas of risk to achieving the purpose. This information is then used to build contingency into the plan in terms of cost and time.

B.4.4 Direct execution of the plan

The manager must provide the staff who carry out the plan with clear and unambiguous statements of what they are to do. These may be in the form of terms of reference or work packet definitions (depending on the level of task). Reporting requirements must also be specified.

B.4.5 Monitor results of execution

Monitoring the effects of the execution of a plan allows the manager to take any informed corrective action. The parameters which are monitored are called control measures (or, simply, measures). The manager obtains current values of these parameters through reports.

Since these measures are the way a manager assesses performance, they can strongly influence an individual's behaviour. Managers should take care to align measures with the desired end so that achievement of the target values of the measures produces the desired result. Parameters must be:

* measurable without undue difficulty or expense

* relevant in demonstrating how well the task is going

* reliable and consistent indicators.

B.4.5.1 Monitoring the external environment

Monitoring changes in the external environment allows:

* re-evaluation of the current plans since assumptions were made about the environment when plans were last modified

* assessment of success or otherwise in executing the plan and in achieving the external elements of the purpose.

Examples of measures relating to the external environment for an IT Services Organization are:

* the rate of transactions by a customer using a service

* the average response time achieved

* income generated by the IT Directorate.

B.4.5.2 Monitoring internal resources

Monitoring internal resources (staff, infrastructure, finance, etc) allows:

* effective utilization of the resources

* redirection of resources to meet the plan

* identification of the need to increase or improve resources (eg training for staff)

* adjustment in the basis of estimates for future planning.

Examples of measures relating to internal resources include:

* productivity (of staff)

* costs incurred

* utilization of capacity (of central processing units, disc storage, etc).

Some measures may relate to different aspects of the same process. An example of this in the delivery of IT services is the average response time achieved by a customer using a service. This is a measure of the external environment because the effect is observed externally by the customer, but it is closely linked to the utilization of computer and communications systems which are measures of internal resources.

B.4.6 Compare results with plans

Monitoring the current situation (both the external environment and the internal resources) allows managers to compare the actual execution with their plans. The identification of deviations from plan is the key to successful control.

Monitoring trends over time provides additional useful information. This trend analysis can detect creeping growth in demand or a gradual deterioration in a resource. It may indicate potential problems which can be rectified before they represent a serious threat.

Trend analysis can be used to modify the time and resource estimates of future activities and tasks - to develop forecasts of future progress based on experience to date. However, these forecasts must overlay forecasts derived from knowledge or prediction of new future requirements.

B.4.7 Decide on corrective action

Corrective action should begin where there is any deviation from plans. There are two types of corrective action:

* modifying plans (the events or their effects cannot be accommodated in the current plans and the plans must be changed)

* implementing changes (the events or their effects need to be accommodated by changing the resources allocated).

The effects of the proposed changes should be considered in terms of overall scheduling and resource management before any changes are made. If the changes require additional resources outside the authority of the manager, management must be advised by report which should include at least one proposed solution.

B.4.8 Report on achievements against plan

Reports are prepared for two purposes:

*   for managers themselves to monitor execution and compare against the plan (B.4.5 and B.4.6)

*   for managers to pass on to higher managers to report on the achievement of purpose.

In each case, reports must be provided at sufficiently timely intervals to allow corrective action, if necessary. They should also be concise and consistent in format.

Whatever their purpose, reports can be of two types:

*   routine reports, which present only information on progress as part of the overall planning and control activity

*   exception reports, which present information to highlight a problem and the need for corrective action from management.

B.5 Strategic planning

Strategic planning is the process of identifying the longer term objectives of an organization and deciding how they will be achieved.

The strategic planning horizon is relatively long, typically between three and ten years. The range depends on the type of business. Because of the long timescale, the level of detail developed on how to achieve the objectives is relatively low. Strategic planning is normally conducted as a review and update of previous plans every one or two years. It must specify:

*   the direction of the organization through

    -   mission

    -   vision

    -   values

* the reasons and assumptions on which this direction is based

* the processes and activities that must be initiated to achieve the objectives stated in corporate business and IS strategy plans.

Because of the long timescale the question of how the organization reaches its goals is only considered in terms of the approximate costs, timescales and resources required. The uncertainties and risks need to be assessed and expressed in qualitative terms or as policy decisions.

Most large organizations are structured on a hierarchical basis. Each part of the organization has objectives based on the business strategy but focussed on its own particular product or functional responsibility.

Mission | The organization may have a succinct statement of its purpose. This is the mission and is the highest form of direction provided. Typically, mission statements state why the organization is in business, but include little or no detail of how business is to be conducted.

Vision | An organization's vision is its statement of what it intends to be in the future. The vision statement contains targets for size, range of services, or geographic coverage, for instance.

Values | Organizations have a preferred way of doing business which supports their cultural and commercial goals. This preference is usually embodied in a set of values which are expressed as broad statements reflecting the organization's attitudes and beliefs. Values give clear guidance to all managers on how the organization wishes to do business.

B.6 Tactical planning

Tactical planning builds detail on to the strategic plans and develops plans of action for more immediate timescales, typically for the next 12-18 months.

Tactical plans take into account available resources, staff and current commitments to define how the strategic goals will be met within existing constraints. In addition, they identify what resource, staffing, process and supporting infrastructure changes are necessary.

Tactical planning results in two types of plan:

* plans which define how resources will be used to support an ongoing commitment

* plans which relate to programmes for the development of business and infrastructure.

B.7 Operational planning

Operational planning takes tactical plans down to a detailed level suitable for directing and monitoring activities on a day-to-day basis.

Operational plans cover a single project or a function such as cost management or the Capacity Planning function in the IT Services Organization. They generally cover a period of up to a year (very long projects may be divided into phases each with its own operational plan). Typically for a function the plan covers the financial year.

Operational plans may vary in detail over the planning period. Plans for the final quarter in the period may be in outline only when they are first developed but as this particular quarter gets closer and uncertainties are resolved, more detail can be added.

Planning and control for operational purposes is very specific to the task in hand although it can be seen to follow the general principles behind any planning and control activity which were described in section B.4.

B.8 Business planning

Business planning is the process of putting in place the means to achieve business strategy. It takes place in four stages:

* Business Direction, charting the objectives and the critical success factors which will ensure attainment of the objectives

* Business Processes, examining how the organization is set up to achieve its goals

* Business Resources, including staff, financial assets and information technology, to see how well these resources support the business processes

* Business Programmes, which are designed to implement some change in a combination of direction, process or resource.

Business planning takes into account the opportunities in the market and the capabilities and resources of the organization. These are then reconciled to decide on the best course of action. This results in plans that focus effort in a common direction to achieve the overall business strategy.

Planning must be based on realistic and practical assessments of both the customer base and the capabilities of the organization. IS staff involvement in business planning is crucial for the successful exploitation of technology.

External factors such as changes by business competitors, changes in the economic climate and legislation and advances in technology all affect how an organization conducts business. Significant changes affect existing plans which must be changed to match the new circumstances.

B.9 Planning and control as part of a Quality Management System

A basic requirement of an organization is a Quality Management System (QMS). An essential part of the QMS is an effective mechanism to plan and control all business activities, including the provision of IT services. This ensures a consistent approach and provides an opportunity for improving the planning and control process which, in turn, will improve the ability to meet the organization's mission.

A formal management system to support the Planning and Control function makes it possible to extract additional information which relates to the planning and control process itself. This allows managers to improve aspects such as forecasting, estimating resource requirements and quality control.

Annex C. IS and IT planning

This annex summarizes CCTA's guidance on planning for Information Systems (IS). More detail is available in the IS Guides, which are the source material for the annex. This annex:

*   introduces the topic of IS planning(C.1)

*   describes the recommendations for a management framework for IS planning (C.2)

*   describes IS strategy planning (C.3)

*   describes IT infrastructure planning (C.4).

C.1 Information Systems planning

The identification of business requirements for IS occurs in the business planning stages. It involves deciding how the business operations are to be carried out and what information, and therefore IS, is required to support them. Strategic planning for information systems is primarily the responsibility of business managers who must specify their information needs clearly.

Identifying these information requirements depends on an understanding of the value of information to the business and on an understanding of what opportunities are available through the use of IT. CCTA recommends the use of teams from a mixture of backgrounds (eg IT, business and consultants) as the best means of staffing a group for IS planning.

The information needs of the business activities define the requirements for IT services. By analysis of the use of the information, service priorities can be defined.

The requirements should be expressed in business terms before any technical solution has been considered. By defining the requirements in this way the IT Services Manager can be sure that the service requirements stated are business requirements.

Once defined, service requirements should be expressed as Service Level Agreements (SLAs) which form a 'contract' between the business customer and the IT services supplier. See the IT Infrastructure Library **Service Level Management** module.

Information systems analysis studies can be used to identify opportunities for improving business operations. By analyzing business processes and information flows and processing, the cost and quality of information systems can be greatly improved.

More importantly, by developing a better understanding of how and why the business uses the information and its value, the service level requirements and their relative business priorities can be better understood. This leads to a better match between the IS service provided and the business needs.

C.2 Management framework for IS planning

CCTA recommends that IS planning is conducted within a formal management framework. The key elements involved are summarized below, and are taken from the IS Guides and the recent work in CCTA on Methods Harmonization and on Infrastructure Planning. The management framework is depicted at figure 2 (page 16).

Management Board and Business Planners

These are at the top of the parent organization and generate business strategy and business plans. They are the ultimate customers for the IT Services Organization.

The IS Steering Committee (ISSC)

The ISSC reports to the parent organization's management board and is responsible for setting the parent organization's Information Systems strategy.

IS Planning Secretariat (ISPS)

The ISPS supports the ISSC, coordinates the activities of the various Executive Committees with those of the ISSC and acts as guardian of the IS strategy.

Programmes and Projects

Programmes are derived from business plans and strategy which they are designed to implement. Implementation is by means of a collection of projects some or all of which may have an IT component. A Programme Director represents the parent organization and ensures the parent organization obtains its expected business benefit from the programme. The Programme Director is supported by a Programme Executive which includes the Programme Manager.

Programme and project plans are maintained by the Project Support Office (PSO) on behalf of the managers. The IT Services Manager should be represented at meetings which discuss and review these plans where the provision of IT services or the development and operation of IT infrastructure are involved. The IT Services Organization should obtain copies of relevant plans from the PSO.

The development of new software may be undertaken by the parent organization itself or it may be procured from external suppliers. More guidance is available in the CCTA IT Infrastructure Library **Software Lifecycle Support** module.

IT Executive Committee (ITEC)

The ITEC is responsible for the IT components which meet the IS Strategy. It is normally chaired by the IT Director.

Project Support Office (PSO) and IT Planning Unit (ITPU)

The planning and control process produces a significant amount of information which must be analyzed, documented, and made easily accessible. This includes the consolidation of information across projects and activities for use in forecasting and performance measurement by, for example, function, resource or achievement of a milestone.

Many organizations set up a group to support these related management control activities and IT services support activities. The group may be:

* a Project Support Office (PSO), which usually supports new system development projects

* an IT Planning Unit (ITPU), which supports the ITEC. The ITPU can also be used to support IT Services Organization activities.

The ITPU must interface with other planning functions that share the same aim of delivering, managing and controlling effectively the organization's investment in IS. The ITPU must interface with:

* those responsible for the IS Strategy for particular business areas

* those responsible for the Corporate IS Strategy

* the PSO, if the organization is large enough to warrant a separate PSO

* individual IT Services Organization planners.

The role of the ITPU is explained in a CCTA IS Planning Subject Guide entitled The Role of the IT Planning Unit.

The ITPU is responsible to the ITEC for the planning activities within the IT Directorate in response to the demands of the business which are expressed through strategies and business plans. Its activities can be summarized to include:

* administrative and clerical support

* support documentation library

* resource scheduling and management

* coordination of management information

* performance measurement

* financial monitoring.

The head of the ITPU acts as a suitable point for planning teams to reconcile their conflicting priorities and resource requirements with the overall business need.

The IT Directorate

The IT Directorate is responsible for the IT infrastructure, the provision of IT services and, often, the development of new applications.

The IT Directorate must provide assistance to business managers in producing their IS plans. To give effective assistance, IT Directorate staff must concentrate on the information and business issues and not on possible IT based solutions.

The IT Services Manager

The IT Services Manager is responsible to the IT Director for ensuring that IT services meet the customer's needs both now and in the future. To do this, the IT Services Manager must clearly understand the customer's current requirements and have some understanding of how they will develop in the future. This can only be achieved by understanding, in detail, the business use and value of the various aspects of the IT services provided, in the customer's terms.

C.3 The IS strategy planning process

The IS Strategy Plan should provide clear direction on the services the IT infrastructure will supply to meet the needs of the business for the foreseeable future. The plan considers the business conditions and IS conditions and how these will shape the business demands for information systems.

Business conditions

Current and future business conditions are considered in terms of how they may affect the business requirements for IS. This means quantifying the likelihood of changes in business priorities and methods of working in the organization. Similarly, financial and other resource constraints must be defined.

Much of this information is available from the business strategy plans. However, the implications for IS need careful evaluation.

IS conditions

Current IS conditions, including existing plans, require careful consideration. An understanding of the current position provides valuable information on the constraints placed on existing and future strategies.

The planning process produces options for future IS strategies. These options must be examined to identify the business and the IS implications of each scenario considered.

From these analyses, organizations can reach decisions as to what is expected from the IT Directorate during the planned period. With final management agreement the planning team can convert the decisions into an outline plan for progressing any agreed strategies.

Many important decisions are made as a result of the IS strategy study. It is important to document the basis for these decisions and to make this information available to managers and planners responsible for subsequently implementing the plan. The role of tactical planning is to determine how the IT Directorate will supply the systems and services to meet the business demands identified by the strategy study.

An IS strategic planning exercise typically consists of the five phases:

* scoping study

* strategy study

* strategy definition

* implementation planning

* monitoring, tuning and review.

Scoping study

The study defines the breadth of the strategic planning exercise and identifies any issues which must be addressed before the strategy study can start. The study identifies how many strategies the organization needs.

Strategy study

The strategy study takes account of existing business reports, strategies, policies and business plans. From these the planning team derives a series of business objectives and priorities. Current business operations are usually modelled in some detail including details of the information requirements. This activity should involve the IT Services Organization and provides insight into how IT can be best utilized. A detailed appraisal of current application services and costs is also included.

From this analysis, a series of options or scenarios are identified. These are then evaluated in terms of the potential costs and benefits to the business. Business Objectives and Business Priorities documents are produced during this phase. These documents are of particular importance for subsequent planning and management purposes. The documents detail what the goals are and provide a weighted priority for each objective.

Strategy definition

During the strategy definition phase the options chosen are developed into an outline portfolio of work. Estimates are made of the resources required and the business benefits that will accrue. This includes an evaluation of how the existing infrastructure will migrate to meet the new requirements.

Management and technical policies are formalized and documented at this time. However, additional work may be required subsequently before policies are finalized.

Implementation planning

The decisions and supporting documentation from strategic planning are passed to the tactical planning teams who are responsible for developing programmes into detailed implementation project proposals.

A plan is drawn up for the required work programme. This plan must take into account lead times for procurement, resource limitations and interdependencies. Individual project profiles will take account of resources, funding and benefits.

A proposed programme of work is produced, based on a realistic assessment of what is possible given the current priorities and constraints. Where conflicts arise between business priorities and the programme order, the reasons for these must be highlighted to senior management. Where possible these should be accompanied by ideas for overcoming such problems and their impact on the budget and timescales.

Monitoring, tuning and review

This is a continuing activity whose objectives are to ensure that the strategy delivers the expected business benefits.

C.4 IT infrastructure planning

Business and technology are in a constant state of change. The rate of technological advancement in the computer and telecommunications industries is high. This rapidly changes the investment options available and poses difficulties for the IS strategy planner. By choosing inappropriate technologies for hardware, software and network services in the long term the IT Services Planner could significantly constrain the organization's growth, and technologies may be difficult to change.

IS strategy planning must address the IT needs of the organization for the strategic planning period. This is an important consideration for the business.

The ideal situation is where the application systems and supporting data can be supported on a wide range of technology without significant change or dependence on specific systems.

Infrastructure planning turns the programme or programmes that emerge from the strategic planning exercise, to add new or to enhance existing IT services in

support of changing business needs, into a set of projects.
The process makes a more detailed assessment of the actual
resources available and current constraints and risks. The
emphasis is on what will be delivered and the infrastructure
changes necessary to support these deliverables.

The limitations on resources must be resolved during
tactical planning. These limitations may be due to current
commitments, such as maintaining existing services and
existing development projects, or financial constraints.

Final arbitration of what is to be achieved will be decided
by the business priorities established during strategic
planning.

Extended table of contents

Annex D. Description of documents

This annex describes the documents which are concerned with planning and control for IT services. The documents are categorized under section headings referenced below.

Purpose (D.1)

These documents, delivered by the parent organization, define what is required of the IT Services Organization. They cover the following aspects (which are explained more fully in Annex B, section B.3):

* mission

* plans and requirements

* corporate policies, procedures, standards and guidelines.

External (D.2)

Documents from outside the parent organization which influence or constrain the way the IT Services Organization can work.

IT Services Organization

In performing planning and control, the IT Services Organization produces plans, specifications, procedures and reports which are described in the following categories:

Top level plans, specifications reports and procedures (D.3)
Operational plans for service provision (D.4)
Operational plans for infrastructure management (D.5)
Internal service provision reports (D.6)
Internal infrastructure management reports (D.7).

In the document definitions the following structure is used:

m.n Document title

"m.n" is the document reference used throughout this module.

Source

The originator of a document.

Description

A summary of the document.

Dependencies

Any other documents needed in order to produce it.

References

Elaboration on the purpose and content of the document. This is a reference to a section of Annex E of this module or to other publications which contain further guidance. The IT Infrastructure Library modules and other CCTA books given as references may not use the same title as that used in this annex, or indeed use any title, to identify the document whose purpose is described here.

D.1 Purpose

1.1 Terms of Reference for IT Services Organization

Source	Parent organization (ISSC) via the IT Directorate.
Description	A definition of the scope of activities and the responsibilities of the IT Services Organization identifying customers to be served and accountability to the parent organization.
Dependencies	Business plans.
References	Annex E, section E.1.

1.2 IS Strategy Study Report

Source	Parent organization (ISSC).
Description	The strategic direction for the use of IS in the parent organization covering:

* the contribution of IS to the business

* IS management, staffing and financing issues

* policies for infrastructure procurement, information management, systems development and systems architecture

* plans for future development with cost/benefit justification.

Dependencies	Business plans.
References	CCTA IS Guide A2: Strategic Planning for Information Systems, (Annex B).

1.3 Financial Provisions

Source	Parent organization via the IT Directorate.
Description	The financial resources available to the IT Services Organization to provide the IT services required - normally presented in government departments as the Public Expenditure Survey (PES) Provision and Current Year Budget.
Dependencies	Not applicable.
References	IT Infrastructure Library Module: Cost Management for IT Services.

1.4   Programme Plan

Source   Programme Manager.

Description   Definition of programmes (as a group of projects)
                        specifying business benefits expected and the top-level
                        plans for changes to business processes, organization and
                        infrastructure.

Dependencies   Business plans;
                        IS Strategy Study Report.

References   CCTA An Introduction to Programme Management;
                        A Guide to Programme Management

1.5   Project Plan

Source   Project Manager.

Description   Definition of a project for developing the IT infrastructure,
                        including implementing new applications systems,
                        specifying:

                        *   project objectives

                        *   the programme which the project supports

                        *   activities, time scales, resources, costs

                        *   installation and testing requirements including
                             involvement of the IT Services Organization and
                             needs for user testing.

Dependencies   Programme Plans.

References   IT Infrastructure Library Module: Software Lifecycle
                        Support;
                        IT Infrastructure Library Module: Testing an IT Service for
                        Operational Use (Annex E);
                        PRINCE and SSADM documentation also contain examples
                        relevant to IT projects.

**1.6   Service Level
         Agreement**

Source   IT Services Organization Service Level Management and
                        the Customer.

Description   Definition of the IT services required by a customer
                        detailing standards, capacity limits, performance levels and
                        procedures for review.

Dependencies   Business plans;
                        IT Services Catalogue.

References   IT Infrastructure Library Module: Service Level
                        Management.

1.7 Corporate Policies and Procedures Manual

Source	Parent organization.
Description	Corporate-wide policies and procedures covering

* contingency planning

* accounting for IT services

* quality

* security

* staff employment policies and conditions.

Dependencies	Business plans.
References	CCTA Quality Management Library; CCTA Security Library; CCTA IS Guide C4: Security and Privacy.

D.2 External

2.1 Standard, Regulation or Legislation

Source	Various bodies including British Standards Institution, Government (by Statutory Instrument or other regulations), OFTEL, Commission of the European Community and Data Protection Registrar.
Description	Standards, rules and laws which affect the IT Services Organization and the provision of IT services.
Dependencies	Not applicable.
References	See specific publications.

2.2 Suppliers' Catalogues

Source	Suppliers of goods and services to the IT Services Organization.
Description	A description of products and services available from a supplier defining functionality, physical characteristics, performance, installation requirements and test procedures.
Dependencies	Not applicable.
References	See any hardware or software suppliers information sheets.

D.3 IT Services Organization top level plans, specifications, reports and procedures

3.1 Specification of Requirements for IT Services Organization

Source	IT Services Management Team (using documents described in D.1).
Description	Compilation of what is required of, and of limitations constraining, the IT Services Organization as the basis of all internal planning activity and comprising:

* Terms of Reference for IT Services Organization

* IS Strategy Study Report

* Financial Provisions

* Programme and Project Plans

* Service Level Agreements

* Corporate Policies and Procedures Manual.

Dependencies	The documents listed above.
References	Annex E, section E.2.

3.2 IT Services Organization Strategic Plan

Source	IT Services Management Team
Description	The long term plan of the IT Services Organization for the provision of IT services to its customers showing objectives with targets for the development of resources and attainment of performance measures.
Dependencies	Terms of Reference for IT Services Organization; IS Strategy Study Report.
References	Annex E, section E.3.

**3.3   IT Services Provision
Plan**

Source   IT Services Management Team.

Description   The plan defining how the requirements for IT services will
                            be met by the IT Services Organization based on the Quality
                            Plan - mainly a compilation of operational plans:

*   Customer Support Plan

*   Contingency Plan

*   Security Implementation Plan and Audit Schedule

*   Application Implementation Support Plan

*   Availability Plan

*   Capacity Plan.

Dependencies   Specification of Requirements for IT Services.

References   Annex E, section E.4.

3.4   Service Catalogue

Source   IT Services Organization Service Level Management.

Description   A description of the services offered by the IT Services
                            Organization detailing functionality, operational
                            information, performance, charges.

Dependencies   Specification of Requirements for IT Services;
                            IT Services Provision Plan

References   IT Infrastructure Library Module: Service Level
                            Management.

**3.5   IT Services
Infrastructure Plan**

Source   IT Services Management Team.

Description   Definition of how the IT infrastructure will be used to
                            deliver the IT Services Provision Plan and comprising:

*   Change Plan

*   Financial Plan

*   QMS Amendment Plan and Audit Schedule

*   Staff Plan

*   Operations Plan

	*	Configuration Plan
	*	Environmental Plan.

Dependencies	Specification of Requirements for IT Services; IT Services Provision Plan.
References	Annex E, section E.5.

3.6 Service Level Performance Report

Source	IT Services Organization Service Level Management.
Description	A comparison of the actual service performance delivered to a customer against the requested service level documented in the Service Level Agreement and advance warning of future variations in performance level (eg planned system downtime) or special requests for assistance (eg user testing of new applications) or report on progress against IT project plans.
Dependencies	Service Level Agreement; Project Plan; Change Plan; Application Implementation Support Plan.
References	IT Infrastructure Library Module: Service Level Management.

3.7 IT Services Organization Report

Source	IT Services Manager
Description	The high level report to the IT Directorate indicating the actual status of all major measures of performance versus the planned and forecast values detailing significant achievements and explaining major variations.
Dependencies	All operation level status and performance reports and plans.
References	Annex E, section E.6.

3.8 **IT Services Organization Management Report**

      Source   IT Services Organization Planning and Control.

      Description   Status report for the IT Services Management Team summarising the situation across functional areas of the IT Services Organization.

      Dependencies   All operational level plans, status and performance reports.

      References   Annex E, section E.7.

3.9 **Request For Change**

      Source   IT Services Management Team or individual function.

      Description   Specification of a requested change to the IT Services Organization's plans relating to IT services provision, IT infrastructure, or its own organization or procedures.

      Dependencies   Not applicable.

      References   IT Infrastructure Library Module: Change Management, (Annex E).

3.10 **IT Services Organization Quality Management System**

      Source   IT Services Management Team.

      Description   Definition of the policies and management procedures in the IT Services Organization covering the IT Services Organization's functions including planning and control.

      Dependencies   Corporate Policies and Procedures Manual; IT Services Organization Strategic Plan.

      References   IT Infrastructure Library Module: Quality Management for IT Services.

D.4 Operational plans for service provision

4.1 Customer Support Plan

Source	IT Services Organization's Service Level Management.
Description	Plan of how a specified customer will be supported for a given future period detailing:

* known customer requirements, now and into the future, extracted from SLA and discussions with customer

* delivery requirements on the infrastructure, especially for availability, capacity, contingency and operational support.

Dependencies	Specification of Requirements for IT Services.
References	Annex E, section E.8.

4.2 Contingency Plan

Source	IT Services Organization Contingency Management.
Description	The plan of all activities necessary to provide essential IT services in the event of a disaster affecting the IT infrastructure detailing an implementation plan, IT infrastructure, staff and standby facilities required, management and operational policies, security, requisites for terminating disaster status - based on organization's security and contingency policies.
Dependencies	Corporate Policies and Procedures Manual; Specification of Requirements for IT Services; IT Services Provision Plan; Customer Support Plan.
References	IT Infrastructure Library Module: Contingency Planning (Annex A).

4.3 Availability Plan

Source	IT Services Organization Availability Management.
Description	Definition of the intended availability of the IT infrastructure detailing hours of service, maximum outages, changes to availability, maintenance plans.
Dependencies	Service Level Agreements; Customer Support Plan; Capacity Plan.
References	IT Infrastructure Library Module: Availability Management (Section 3).

4.4 Capacity Plan

Source   IT Services Organization Capacity Management.

Description   Definition of current and expected capacity requirements for all main elements of the IT infrastructure detailing for each resource the current and future installed capacity, usable capacity and expected usage.

Dependencies   Service Level Agreements;
Customer Support Plan;
Availability Plan.

References   IT Infrastructure Library Module: Capacity Management.

4.5 Application Implementation Support Plan

Source   IT Services Organization Applications Development Liaison.

Description   Definition of how the IT Services Organization will support the implementation of new or revised applications software detailing activities, responsibilities, timetable, test measures and needs for user participation.

Dependencies   Project Plan.

References   IT Infrastructure Library Module: Software Lifecycle Support;
IT Infrastructure Library Module: Testing an IT Service for Operational Use.

4.6 Security Implementation Plan and Audit Schedule

Source   IT Services Organization Security Management.

Description   Definition of changes to the physical and data security systems and procedures, and the schedule for security related audits in the IT Services Organization.

Dependencies   Corporate Policies and Procedures Manual;
Specification of Requirements for IT Services;
CRAMM Review of threats and vulnerabilities.

References   CCTA Security Library;
IS Guide C4: Security and Privacy.

D.5 Operational plans for Infrastructure Management

5.1 Configuration Plan

Source	IT Services Organization Configuration Management.
Description	Definition of the IT infrastructure detailing the component items and the procedure for recording changes.
Dependencies	Capacity Plan; Availability Plan; Contingency Plan.
References	IT Infrastructure Library Module: Configuration Management; IT Infrastructure Library Module: Network Management.

5.2 Environmental Plan

Source	IT Services Organization Environmental Management.
Description	Definition of the environmental infrastructure which supports the IT infrastructure specifying the performance and maintenance needs of the component items including power supply, air conditioning, water cooling, physical security, fire detection and suppression provision.
Dependencies	Configuration Plan; Security Implementation Plan and Audit Schedule; Contingency Plan.
References	IS Guide, C2: Environmental Services; IT Infrastructure Library Module: Environmental Services Policy; IT Infrastructure Library Module: Environmental Standards for Equipment Accommodation.

5.3 Operations Plan

Source	IT Services Organization Operations Management.
Description	Schedule and definition of the reactive operational activities that are required to run the IT Services Organization's infrastructure, frequently documented as the Operations Manual, detailing call out procedures, back-up procedures, on-line system procedures, input and output control, etc.
Dependencies	Service Level Agreements; Customer Support Plan; Availability Plan.
References	IT Infrastructure Library Module: Computer Operations Management (Annex C); IT Infrastructure Library Module: Network Services Management.

5.4 Staff Plan

Source   IT Services Organization Staff Management.

Description   Plan for use of staff resources in the IT Services Organization detailing:

* list of staff and their skills (Skills Register)

* numbers (recruitment needs, provision for redundancy or separations)

* schedules for appraisals, pay increases, bonuses

* skills and training needed

* estimates of total staff costs.

Dependencies Corporate Policies and Procedures Manual;
IT Services Provision Plan;
IT Services Infrastructure Plan.

References   IT Infrastructure Library Module: Cost Management for IT Services (Annex E for cost-related parts of plan);
IT Services Organization.

5.5 Financial Plan

Source   IT Services Organization Cost Management.

Description   Annual budgets for the IT Services Organization detailing operating costs, income or cost recovery and capital expenditure.

Dependencies IT Services Provision Plan;
IT Services Infrastructure Plan;
Service Level Agreements;
Customer Support Plan.

References   IT Infrastructure Library Module: Cost Management for IT Services (Annex E).

5.6 Change Plan

Source   IT Services Organization Change Management.

Description   Description and schedule of the major changes to the IT infrastructure in the next one to two years.

Dependencies Specification of Requirements for IT Services;
IT Services Provision Plan;
IT Services Infrastructure Plan.

References   Annex E, section E.9.

5.7 QMS Amendment Plan and Audit Schedule

Source	IT Services Organization Quality Management.
Description	Definition of the required amendments to the IT Services Organization Quality Management System, detailing the schedule of audits.
Dependencies	Corporate Policies and Procedures Manual; IT Services Organization Quality Management System; IT Services Provision Plan; IT Services Infrastructure Plan.
References	IT Infrastructure Library Module: Quality Management for IT Services.

D.6 Internal service provision reports

6.1 Customer Requests Assessment Report

Source	IT Services Organization Service Level Management.
Description	Assessment by the Customer Account Management Group of changes requested by the customer(s) arising from new requirements, increased demand or persistent problems, specifically identifying those changes which require approval by the IT Services Management Team.
Dependencies	Service Level Agreements.
References	ITIL Module: Customer Liaison; ITIL Module: Help Desk; ITIL Module: Service Level Management.

6.2 Problem and User Incident Report

Source	IT Services Organization Problem Management.
Description	A report summarising the levels and business impact of problems and user incidents broken down by each customer and each functional area of the IT Services Organization.
Dependencies	User Incident Reports (from the Help Desk); Problem Reports.
References	IT Infrastructure Library Module: Problem Management (Annex B); IT Infrastructure Library Module: Help Desk (Annex B4).

6.3 Customer Satisfaction Questionnaire

Source	IT Services Organization Service Level Management.
Description	Completed questionnaire indicating the customer's perceptions about the quality of IT services received.
Dependencies	Not applicable.
References	IT Infrastructure Library Module: Customer Liaison (Annex C).

**6.4   Contingency Plan
        Audit Report**

Source	IT Services Organization Contingency Management.
Description	Result of an audit or test of the contingency plans for a given customer, service or facility, detailing compliance with corporate policies and ability to meet specified requirements.
Dependencies	Contingency Plan.
References	IT Infrastructure Library Module: Contingency Planning (section 5.1.4).

**6.5   Capacity
        Performance Report**

Source	IT Services Organization Capacity Management.
Description	Review of the actual usage of IT infrastructure resources against planned and forecast levels.
Dependencies	Capacity Plan.
References	IT Infrastructure Library Module: Capacity Management (Annex L).

**6.6   Security Status
        Report**

Source	IT Services Organization Security Management.
Description	Report on the status of IT Services Organization security management activities including audits.
Dependencies	Security Implementation Plan and Audit Schedule.
References	Annex E, section E.10.

**6.7   Security Audit
        Report**

Source	IT Services Organization Security Management.
Description	The result of a security audit, by an internal or external body, on a part of the IT Services Organization, detailing general status, compliance, failures in compliance, recommended actions.
Dependencies	Security Implementation Plan and Audit Schedule; Corporate Policies and Procedures Manual.
References	CCTA Security Library; IS Guide, C4, Security and Privacy (section 6).

D.7 Internal Infrastructure Management Reports

7.1 Operations Performance Report

Source	IT Services Organization Operations Management.
Description	Review of operational performance of all aspects of the IT infrastructure (including computers, networks and local terminals) covering availability, configuration and environmental measurement, and direct support of end customers.
Dependencies	Operations Plan.
References	IT Infrastructure Library Module: Computer Operations Management (section 5.1.3.1).

7.2 Staff Report

Source	IT Services Organization Staff Management.
Description	Report on the achievement against the Staff Plan highlighting problems.
Dependencies	Staff Plan.
References	None available.

7.3 Financial Performance Report

Source	IT Services Organization Cost Management.
Description	Summary of financial performance of the IT Services Organization against planned and forecast.
Dependencies	Financial Plan; Actual costs.
References	IT Infrastructure Library Module: Cost Management for IT Services (Annex E).

**7.4   Change Management
Report**

Source   IT Services Organization Change Management.

Description   Report on the achievement against the planned changes
                           detailing:

                           *   the number of requests for change received

                           *   progress in implementing changes

                           *   the costs associated with processing them

                           *   summary of impact on IT services provision.

Dependencies   Change Plan.

References   IT Infrastructure Library Module: Change Management.

7.5   Quality Status Report

Source   IT Services Organization Quality Management.

Description   Report on the status of quality management activities and
                           performance against plan.

Dependencies   QMS Amendment Plan and Audit Schedule.

References   Annex E, section E.10.

7.6   Quality Audit Report

Source   IT Services Organization Quality Management.

Description   Result of a quality audit (internal or by an external body) on
                           part of the IT Services Organization detailing general status,
                           compliance against Quality Management System, failures in
                           compliance and recommended actions.

Dependencies   Corporate Policies and Procedures Manual;
                           QMS Amendment and Audit Schedule.

References   CCTA Quality Management Library;
                           IT Infrastructure Library Module: Quality Management for
                           IT Services.

7.7   Report on Performance of Supplier

Source	IT Services Organization Supplier Liaison.
Description	An assessment of the current performance of a supplier and its products and services, including maintenance.
Dependencies	Reports from IT Services Organization functions on supplied products and services.
References	IT Infrastructure Library Module: Managing Supplier Relationships; IT Infrastructure Library Module: Third Party and Single Source Maintenance (section 5.1.2).

7.8   Supplier Rating

Source	IT Services Organization Supplier Liaison.
Description	Overall assessment of a supplier to the IT Services Organization to comply with quality management requirements and to help set supplier selection policies.
Dependencies	Report on Performance of Supplier.
References	IT Infrastructure Library Module: Managing Supplier Relationships.

7.9   Planning and Control Status Report

Source	IT Services Organization Planning and Control Management.
Description	Report on performance of the planning and control system including statistics, trends and forecasts.
Dependencies	Defined planning and control system.
References	This IT Infrastructure Library Module (section 4.1.3).

Annex E. Contents of documents

This annex provides more detail on some of the documents described in Annex D. The document reference in Annex D appears in brackets after each document title. The document frameworks given are not necessarily comprehensive but are proposed as a basis on which organizations can build their own documents.

E.1 Terms of Reference for IT Services Organization (1.1)

This document is a statement of the overall purpose of the IT Services Organization within the IT Directorate. It establishes the scope of operations and responsibilities for the group.

Mission

Example: "To provide cost effective infrastructure services to the customers in North West Division".

Definition of customers

Either a generic way of identification or a list.

Definition of services required

A list of services, with a description of each service required now and in the future, referring to Service Level Agreements.

Responsibility

Example: "Responsible to the IT Director for the operation of networking and central processing support for the business systems required".

Organization

Overview of organization, locations, etc.

E.2 Specification of Requirements for IT Services Organization (3.1)

This document is a comprehensive statement of the requirements to be covered by the IT Services Organization, together with known limitations such as budgets or staffing limits. The document is used as the basis for all internal planning activity.

Definitions and scope

Definition of the planning period (normally 1 to 5 years), and the timetable for progressing the responses to the requirements. IT Services Organization's objectives and terms of reference may be re-stated.

Requirements for IT Services

List of customers.

Current services to customers:

* summary of SLAs

* Service Catalogue.

Future requirements:

* known future demands from existing customers (from SLAs)

* infrastructure projects being implemented in planning period (from Project Plans)

* programmes being progressed in planning period (from Programme Plans)

* applications being implemented in planning period

* known new application requirements.

Constraints on IT Services Organization

* Financial - agreed budget, or statements such as "Total budget not exceeding previous year, increased by Retail Price Index"

* Staff - limitations on staff numbers or targets for staff reduction

* Other resources - changes in available accommodation etc.

E.3 IT Services Organization Strategic Plan (3.2)

All major parts of an organization should have a view or vision of their direction and future. The IT Services Organization should develop and maintain a strategic level plan, charting the intended direction for up to 5 years. This is especially relevant when a number of unrelated customers are supported, as the IT Services Organization will have greater independence and responsibility in the way the total customer requirement is satisfied.

The IT Services Organization Strategic Plan covers the following areas:

* mission

* overall vision

* major directions:

    - predicted requirements

    - architectures and technologies to be deployed

    - benefits expected

* technical policies

* quality policies

* policies for use of standards

* major internal projects (rationalization of data centres or move to distributed processing)

* progress measures and milestones.

E.4 IT Services Provision Plan (3.3)

This plan is built up from many functions within the IT Services Organization. The Specification of Requirements for IT Services identifies the demands on the organization from existing customers, new projects and corporate policies. The following functions must define how the IT Services Organization will provide for those requirements:

* Service Level Management (Customer Support Plan)

* Contingency Planning (Contingency Plan)

* Capacity Management (Capacity Plan)

* Availability Management (Availability Plan)

* Security Management (Security Implementation Plan and Audit Schedule)

* Application Development Liaison (Application Implementation Support Plan).

Each function makes a draft proposal on how to provide the requirements in their area of responsibility, and the Planning and Control function facilitates negotiation to arrive at a draft IT Services Provision Plan. This plan will typically be started before the IT Services Infrastructure Plan, but the two plans should evolve in parallel until a cost effective infrastructure is matched to the service provision.

The Plan will typically include the following information.

Services provided

List of services with descriptions, and mapping of customers to services.

Activities

A list of activities needed to deliver the plan. Activities will be at a higher level than the underlying function plans. Each activity will have a description and any time constraints associated.

Timetable

Schedule of key events.

Resources needed

Definition of and quantity of resources needed to fulfil the plan.

Costs

Financial implications of the plan, including costs and revenues.

Progress measurement

The method used to measure progress against plan.

E.5 IT Services Infrastructure Plan (3.5)

The IT Services Infrastructure Plan defines the hardware and software that is to be provided to support the IT services that customers require. The IT Services Provision Plan is the major input to this, however the two plans are highly inter related and will develop in parallel. The following functions will be involved in the development of this infrastructure plan:

* Cost Management (Financial Plan)

* Change Management (Change Plan)

* Operations (Operations Plan)

* Configuration Management (Configuration Plan)

* Environmental Management (Environmental Plan)

* Staff Management (Staff Plan)

* Quality Management (QMS Amendment Plan and Audit Schedule).

The Planning and Control function facilitates a negotiation between the various functions involved to produce a consistent Infrastructure Plan. Planning and Control also facilitates the interaction between the Infrastructure Plan and Provision Plan to ensure the cost effective support of the services to be provided.

The IT Services Infrastructure Plan typically contains the following information.

Activities

A list of activities needed to deliver the plan. Activities will be at a higher level than the underlying function plans. Each activity will have a description and any constraints on time.

Timetable

Schedule of key events.

Resources needed

Definition of and quantity of resources needed to fulfil the plan.

Costs

Financial implications of the plan, including costs and revenues.

Progress measurement

The method used to measure progress against plan.

E.6 IT Services Organization Report (3.7)

The overall performance of the IT Services Organization is reviewed in many forums. The IT Services Organization Report is the external performance report for line management. It is presented by the IT Services Manager to the IT Directorate. The report is distinct from that used internally by the IT Services Management Team (see below).

The IT Services Organization Report typically includes the following information.

Report identification

Title, reporting period.

General status

Discussion of general situation, key events, achievements, major issues.

Project updates

IT Services Organization's contribution to projects.

Performance measures

High level summary measures, last period values and trends, for example:

* availability, actual against target

* CPU utilization, actual against target

* major issues and concerns.

Items that require IT Directorate attention

Appendices

Specific reports received in the reporting period such as a Security Audit or Report on Performance of Supplier.

E.7 IT Services Organization Management Report (3.8)

This is the internal version of the IT Services Organization Report. It covers the same topics but at a lower level of detail, enabling functional managers to assess the interactions between their areas of responsibility. The typical contents are as follows.

Report identification

Title, reporting period.

General status

Discussion of general situation, key events and achievements, major issues. Progress on internal projects is also covered.

Project updates

The present status of all IT Services Organization Projects, internal and external.

Performance measures

Individual measures for each function, last period values and trends, for example:

* availability, actual against target

* CPU utilization, actual against target

* major Issues and concerns.

Items that require IT Services Management Team attention.

E.8 Customer Support Plan (4.1)

This document is produced by the Service Level Management function. It covers the plans to support a given customer for the coming year.

Customer

Identification of the customer, by name, locations etc.

Services used

The services used to meet the customers requirements. Details of the use made should be included, for example, ''On-line and Database Processing Services are used for input and enquiries on Certificates''.

If additional services are to be used during the planning period these should be detailed as well, for example, ''From June '94, uninterruptible service will be used for E-Mail''.

Workload prediction

Current workload measurements and forward prediction in terms used for internal planning, for example:

Resource	Q1	Q2	Q3	Q4
Transactions (K/hour)	15	23	22	27
Customer records (Gbytes)	55	90	90	100

Revenue prediction

If costs are recovered on services then predictions of charges to, and therefore revenues from, the customer should be included.

E.9   Change Plan (5.6)

This plan is produced by the Change Management function and is a high level forecast of the major changes to the IT infrastructure and services that will occur in the coming year. This schedule of major events is used:

* as a guide when considering the planning of other changes, hence avoiding conflicts

* to draw together a number of small changes.

For example, introducing a new major application at the same time as a CPU replacement. It is particularly useful when the IT Services Organization supports multiple, unrelated customers.

Timeline

Start and finish of major activities plotted on a timeline for the next year. Each activity is identified with a title or reference (or both), for example:

```
Jan   Feb   Mar   Apr   May   Jun   Jul    etc.


            <==============> (MC/034 - replace ICL CPU)
                <==========> (MC/055 - Install UPS)
                    <==> (MC/090 - Implement CSS2)
```

Major change descriptions

For each change, a description of the change with details of:

* start and finish dates

* probable impact

* dependencies and risks

* comments on how firm the scheduling is.

E.10 General Status Report

Most functions in the IT Services Organization produce a plan of their intended activities. To indicate the progress towards achieving that plan a status report is produced at regular intervals. This report typically contains the following items.

Identification

The function, reporting period, plan being reported against.

General status

Discussion of situation, general progress, major achievements and issues.

Progress measurement

Specific milestones achieved, where applicable.

Performance measurement

Comparisons of the planned and actual values of performance measures. The latest reporting period and the trend should be included, for example:

* actual costs against planned costs

* CPU utilization observed against predicted utilization

* variance explanations should be included

* changes to plan and corrective actions.

Annex F. Directory of functional groups

This directory is arranged by groups of functions (refer to figure 3). The directory contains explanations of the broad roles of the functions in each group and lists and describes each of the constituent functions. The functions within each group are arranged alphabetically. The abbreviation ITIL has been used for the IT Infrastructure Library modules.

F.1 Customers Group

F.1.1 Definition

The Customers Group, which is external to the IT Services Organization, consists of the departmental business functions that require IT services. The customers generally belong to the same parent organization as the IT Services Organization but the information flows are similar if they are outside.

Usually they share a common interest because they are all part of the same organization, but they can also belong to a number of different communities of interest. In each case they benefit through using a single IT Services Organization because they share services or there is benefit through use of the same IT infrastructure.

F.1.2 Constituent Functions

Customer Management

Definition	Representing the departments that are the customers of the IT Services Organization.
ITIL ref	Not applicable - See Customer Account Management (F.9).
Activities	Negotiating SLAs with the IT Services Organization; representing the customers' views.

Users

Definition	The people in the customer departments who use IT services directly.
ITIL ref	Not applicable - See Customer Account Management (F.9) See IS Guide B1.
Activities	Using terminals and other equipment managed by the IT Services Organization; receiving and sending information in electronic or paper form.

F.2 Parent Organization Management Group

F.2.1 Definition

The Parent Organization Management Group embraces all relevant aspects of management within the parent organization to which the IT Services Organization belongs. It includes support functions, such as Finance, as well as the line management directly above the IT Services Organization itself.

Since the functions are outside the IT Services Organization, they are aggregated for simplicity with the information exchanges taking place either through the IT Director (the IT Direction function) or through the function entitled Corporate Bodies which includes Security, Finance, Personnel and so on.

F.2.2 Constituent Functions

Corporate Bodies

Definition	Any department in the parent organization which sets company policies - Personnel, Quality, Security, etc.
ITIL ref	Not applicable.
Activities	Various, but includes setting and promulgating policy.

IT Direction

Definition	Bodies responsible for managing all aspects of the corporate Information Systems (IS) facilities. The direct interface for the IT Services Organization is the IT Director through whom strategy, IS policies, and plans for programmes and projects are passed to enable IT Services Organization's plans to be produced.
ITIL ref	Not applicable - See IS Guides A2 and A3.
Activities	Involved in planning IS Strategy (through membership of IS committees) and managing IS/IT resources. Includes both IT Infrastructure and application work.

F.3 External Group

F.3.1 Definition

This group covers any body outside the parent organization which may have a direct influence on the IT Services Organization.

F.3.2 Constituent Functions

Regulatory Bodies

Definition	Bodies outside the parent organization which constrain or impact the IT Services Organization through law, regulation, audit or other influence. Examples are Data Protection Registrar, Health and Safety Executive and Quality Certification Authorities.
ITIL ref	Not applicable.
Activities	Making and promulgating regulations and standards; checking on conformance to regulation and standards.

Suppliers

Definition	External providers of equipment and services to the IT Services Organization. This is irrespective of whether the IT Services Organization itself is partially or wholly outside the customer parent organization (as it would be in the case of outsourced IT services).
ITIL ref	Managing Supplier Relationships; Third Party and Single Source Maintenance.
Activities	Supply of equipment, software packages, operating software, maintenance, communications lines.

F.4 Internal Suppliers Group

F.4.1 Definition

The Internal Suppliers Group, within the parent organization (usually within the IT Directorate) provides the technical resources of software, hardware and communications which are then used to provide the services to the Customers.

F.4.2 Constituent Functions

Applications Development Management

Definition	Function which manages the provision and maintenance of the application systems. It may use the software development capability of a corporate group or a third party supplier of custom-built applications.

ITIL ref		Software Life Cycle Support.
Activities		Management of analysis, design, construction, implementation and ongoing maintenance.

Procurement

Definition	The function which controls the process of purchasing hardware, packaged software, equipment and services such as maintenance and provision of communications links.
ITIL ref	Managing Supplier Relationships; Computer Installation and Acceptance.
Activities	General relationships with suppliers; identification of suitable products; procurement and price negotiation.

F.5 IT Services Management Group

F.5.1 Definition

This group contains the functions which provide overall management of the IT Services Organization. These functions have roles in coordinating other functions within the IT Services Organization and in interfacing to the Parent Organization Management group.

F.5.2 Constituent Functions

Change Management

Definition	Managing change to the procedures, infrastructure, service provision and plans of the IT Services Organization. This includes the functions of the Change Advisory Board (CAB).
ITIL ref	Change Management.
Activities	Receiving requests for change, determining impact, managing the CAB authorization process and promulgating authorization and implementation details.

Configuration Management

Definition	Manages and controls all aspects of the configuration used to provide the IT services. Covers processing, networking and local equipment.
ITIL ref	Configuration Management; Software Control and Distribution.

Activities	Defines changes to existing configuration to improve performance; identifies new equipment and software needs; maintains configuration records; maintains log of change requests.

Contingency Planning

Definition	Planning for continuance of IT services after disaster or disruption.
ITIL ref	Contingency Planning.
Activities	Determining needs and making, testing and promulgating plans.

Cost Management

Definition	Support to IT Services Organization management on all financial matters.
ITIL ref	Cost Management for IT Services.
Activities	Constructing financial plans and budgets; calculating cost rates for activities and charges for services; recording actual costs and charges.

IT Services Management

Definition	Overall management of the IT Services Organization reporting to the IT Director.
ITIL ref	IT Services Organization; Planning and Control for IT Services.
Activities	Involvement in parent organization's IT planning committees giving advice on aspects relating to IT service provision and infrastructure management; direction to the IT Services Organization; authorization and promulgation of IT Services' plans.

Planning and Control

Definition	Assistance with the establishment and monitoring of IT infrastructure and service provision plans in accordance with IS Strategy; coordination of the IT Services Organization's plans, reporting status and forecasts against plans; identification and reporting of trends.
ITIL ref	Planning and Control for IT Services.
Activities	Identifying constraints and demands from the IS Strategy and Programme Plans; coordinating more detailed planning and publication of the IT Services Infrastructure Plan and IT

Services Provision Plan annually; ongoing monitoring of performance of the IT Services Organization against these plans.

Problem Management

Definition	Dealing with problems (of which the incidents dealt with by the Help Desk are symptoms).
ITIL ref	Problem Management.
Activities	Provision of problem diagnosis and error control; resolution of problems by instigating change; problem prevention; management reporting.

Quality Management

Definition	Ensures management's quality policies are implemented.
ITIL ref	Quality Management for IT Services.
Activities	Maintaining the Quality Management System in accordance with policy; auditing conformance and reporting and advising on deviations.

Security Management

Definition	Ensures management's security policies are implemented.
ITIL ref	Not applicable.
Activities	Auditing adherence to security policy and giving advice to IT Services Organization on meeting the policy.

Staff Management

Definition	Coordination and monitoring of staff matters including recruitment, welfare and training.
ITIL ref	IT Services Organization.
Activities	Keeping staff development plans and records; advising on staff policies; advising on training and career development.

F.6 Supplier's Interface Group

F.6.1 Definition

This group, within the IT Services Organization, manages the acceptance of technical resources (hardware, communications, software and externally supplied services such as communications).

**F.6.2 Constituent
Functions**

**Application
Development Liaison**

Definition	The interface with the Application Development Management function.
ITIL ref	Software Lifecycle Support.
Activities	IT Services Organization's input to application planning; coordination of application requirements; coordination of testing of applications; managing requests for application maintenance due to faults or environmental changes.

Supplier Management

Definition	Management and coordination of relationships with suppliers of goods and services to the IT Services Organization.
ITIL ref	Managing Supplier Relationships.
Activities	Monitoring use of suppliers; monitoring performance of suppliers; arranging for briefings on suppliers' capabilities and products; liaison with contractual/legal and procurement groups; negotiations of call off agreements and high level discounts.

**Testing and
Acceptance**

Definition	Controls the installation and acceptance into productive use of all elements of hardware. Formally tests and accepts new, enhanced and fixed application software, including associated documentation and training, before scheduling for transfer into production.
ITIL ref	Computer Installation and Acceptance; Testing an IT Service for Operational Use.
Activities	For hardware: liaises with suppliers; plans installation; oversees installation activities; tests equipment; generates acceptance certificate; schedules transfer into productive use.
	For software: checks test plans; checks test results; performs additional tests; estimates performance; generates formal acceptance; schedules into production.

F.7 Infrastructure Planning and Management Group

F.7.1 Definition

This group contains the various planning functions which essentially organize the technical resources of hardware, communications and software.

F.7.2 Constituent Functions

Availability Management

Definition	Manages the time periods IT services are provided to customers, and manages the reliability and resilience of the infrastructure which supports those services.
ITIL ref	Availability Management.
Activities	Sets, monitors and controls availability schedules for processing, networks and local equipment.

Capacity Management

Definition	Manages the balance between capacity requirements and capacity provided for aspects of IT services resources.
ITIL ref	Capacity Management; Network Services Management.
Activities	Assessment of practical capacity of installed configuration; definition of capacity measurements; monitoring of actual performance; forward projection of trends; instigating action to correct departures from planned capacity; advice on meeting unexpected workloads; definition of future capacity requirements.

Environmental Management

Definition	Manages all elements of the facilities that house and support the IT Services Organization's operation.
ITIL ref	Environmental Strategy Set, Office Environment Set, Environmental Management Set.
Activities	Defines equipment needed to provide heat, cooling, air-conditioning, power supply to computer and office environments in IT services; monitors achievement of this objective and instigates corrective action to meet failures.

F.8 Infrastructure Operations and Support Group

F.8.1 Definition

This group is responsible for operating the technical resources of the IT Services Organization in order that services may be provided effectively and thereby delivered to the customers. This includes operation of computers, local equipment and networks.

F.8.2 Constituent Functions

Operations

Definition

Regular operation of the infrastructure to provide central processing facilities. Management of equipment on user sites used to provide the IT services. Regular operation of the networking elements of the IT services infrastructure.

ITIL ref

Computer Operations Management;
Unattended Operations;
Management of Local Processors and Terminals;
Network Services Management.

Activities

Daily operations, planning and control of maintenance including third party maintenance; unattended operations; output distribution; schedule of staff and technical resources; daily operation of local equipment; liaison with users on operational matters; monitoring availability and performance.

Technical Support and Coordination

Definition

Implementation of changes and fixes to all elements of the IT infrastructure.

ITIL ref

Not applicable.

Activities

Dealing with technical questions from within the IT Services Organization; implementing changes to IT infrastructure; identifying and applying fixes and work rounds.

F.9 Customer Account Management Group

F.9.1 Definition

The Customer Account Management Group is the part of the IT Services Organization which is responsible for ensuring that customers' needs for services are met. It covers negotiation of Service Level Agreements for current and future requirements, support and dealing with reported user incidents and enquiries.

F.9.2 Constituent Functions

Help Desk

Definition
Single point of contact for operational queries.

ITIL ref
Help Desk.

Activities
Answering queries; recording details of reported user incidents; initiating corrective action where appropriate; reporting status to users and producing statistics on Help Desk work pattern.

Service Level Management

Definition
Interface with the customer departments.

ITIL ref
Customer Liaison;
Service Level Management.

Activities
Negotiating SLAs and liaising with customers to ensure needs are met in accordance with the needs of the parent organization; maintaining Service Catalogue and determining cost of delivery; promotion of service and management of delivery; packaging IT resources as a service with training courses, user manuals and management processes (eg maintaining directories).

CCTA hopes that you find this book both useful and interesting. We will welcome your comments and suggestions for improving it.
Please use this form or a photocopy, and continue on a further sheet if needed.

From:

Name

Organization

Address

Telephone

COVERAGE
Does the material cover your needs?
If not, then what additional material would you like included.

CLARITY
Are there any points which are unclear?
If yes, please detail where and why.

ACCURACY
Please give details of any inaccuracies found.

If more space is required for these or other comments, please continue overleaf.

OTHER COMMENTS

Return to: **Information Systems Engineering Group**
                    CCTA
                    Rosebery Court
                    St Andrews Business Park
                    NORWICH, NR7 0HS

Further information

Further information on the contents of this module can be obtained from:

Information Systems Engineering Group
OGC
Rosebery Court
St Andrews Business Park
NORWICH, NR7 0HS

Telephone: 01603 704704
(GTN: 3040 4704)

Printed in the United Kingdom for The Stationery Office
TJ004093 4/01 C3 10170